P9-DFU-904

DORLING KINDERSLEY ▣ EYEWITNESS BOOKS

AFRICA

Throwing knives, Congo (left) and Gabon (right)

Ancestor figure, Yoruba, Nigeria

Masquerade costume, Chokwe, Angola

Carved elephant tusk, Zulu, South Africa

War shield, Maasai, Kenya

Bronze bells, Benin city, Nigeria

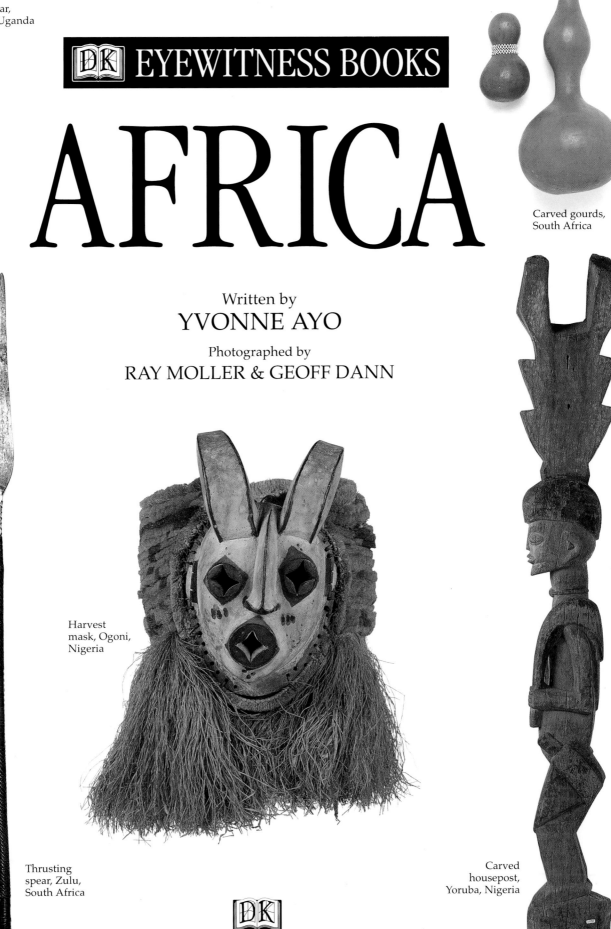

War spear,
Lango, Uganda

DK EYEWITNESS BOOKS

AFRICA

Carved gourds,
South Africa

Written by
YVONNE AYO

Photographed by
RAY MOLLER & GEOFF DANN

Harvest
mask, Ogoni,
Nigeria

Thrusting
spear, Zulu,
South Africa

Carved
housepost,
Yoruba, Nigeria

DK
Dorling Kindersley

Divination staff,
Mozambique

Dance staff,
Nigeria

DK

Dorling Kindersley

LONDON, NEW YORK, AUCKLAND, DELHI, JOHANNESBURG,
MUNICH, PARIS and SYDNEY

Flywhisk,
Nigeria

For a full catalog, visit

DK www.dk.com

Gold weights,
Asante, Ghana

Project editor Miranda Smith
Art editor Vicky Wharton
Managing editor Gillian Denton
Managing art editor Julia Harris
Researcher Céline Carez
Production Catherine Semark
Picture research Deborah Pownell
Editorial consultants Dr John Mack and John Picton
Additional special photography David Garner

This Eyewitness ® Book has been conceived by
Dorling Kindersley Limited and Editions Gallimard

© 1995 Dorling Kindersley Limited
This edition © 2000 Dorling Kindersley Limited
First American edition, 1995

Published in the United States by
Dorling Kindersley Publishing, Inc.
375 Hudson Street,
New York, NY 10014
8 10 9 7

Ceremonial
dagger, Asante,
Ghana

Dorling Kindersley books are available at special discounts for bulk purchases for
sales promotions or premiums. Special editions, including personalized covers,
excerpts of existing guides, and corporate imprints can be created in large quantities
for specific needs. For more information, contact Special Markets Dept., Dorling
Kindersley Publishing, Inc.

Secret society
figures, Yassi,
Sierra Leone

Library of Congress Cataloging-in-Publication Data
Ayo, Yvonne.
Africa / written by Yvonne Ayo;
photography by Geoff Dann, David Garner, and Ray Moller.
p. cm. — (Eyewitness Books)
1. Africa — History — Juvenile Literature.
2. Africa — Social life and customs — Juvenile literature.
[1. Africa — History. 2. Africa — Social life and customs.] I. Title.
DT22.A96 2000   95-2638
960—dc20
ISBN 0-7894-6031-9 (pb)
ISBN 0-7894-6030-0 (hc)

Color reproduction by Colourscan, Singapore
Printed in China by Toppan Printing Co. (Shenzhen) Ltd.

Ceremonial
sword, Asante,
Ghana

Beaded belt, Zulu, South Africa

Contents

Gold trophy head,
Asante, Ghana

A land of contrasts

AFRICA IS A VAST CONTINENT, 5,000 miles (8,000 km) north to south, and over 4,600 miles (7,600 km) across at its widest point. It is a land of deserts, savanna, high mountain ranges, and dense, equatorial forests. Its peoples have been in contact with traders and slavers from Europe, India, and the Far East, as well as with the world religions of Islam and Christianity. More than 1,000 languages are spoken, and there are many different social systems. Yet, for thousands of years, the way of life of many Africans has changed very little. Traditionally, African peoples have made their living by herding, hunting, or farming. African religions, art, and culture reflect these lifestyles, and outside influences are adapted and incorporated.

LIFE ON THE EDGE OF A DESERT
There are two great deserts on the African continent, the Sahara in the north (above) and the Kalahari in the south. In prehistoric times much of these desert areas was fertile, but gradually they have become dry, sandy regions. The lack of regular rainfall makes the life of shepherds and herdspeople of the desert very precarious.

Map drawn by Ortelius in 1570, from information brought back by early explorers

EARLY JOURNEYS
Europeans first heard of Africa's natural resources from Arab geographers. In the 14th century, the arrival of the king of Mali in Cairo carrying gold made the Europeans even more curious. Looking for a sea route to India, Portuguese explorers first sailed around the southern tip of the continent in 1497 and arrived on the east African coast.

HOW THE MAP LOOKS TODAY
Over the centuries, the political and geographical boundaries have continually been altered. Wars of conquest and colonization have remade the map of Africa over and over again. Even today, civil wars in some African countries may change it once again. Names of countries have changed as well. In the 1970s, the new president of the former French colony of Dahomey renamed it the People's Republic of Benin. But the city of Benin which flourished in the 1600s and is famous for its bronzes (pp. 54–55), is now part of modern Nigeria.

THE PROS AND CONS OF TOURISM
The savannas of east Africa are still home to many of the world's most spectacular species of animals. This is largely due to the development of game parks, established nearly 100 years ago to protect the animals from big game hunting. Unfortunately, the Maasai, whose cattle have wandered across the Maasai Mara plains of Kenya (left) for centuries, can no longer follow this lifestyle or hunt wild game.

Figures are carved in wood and painted

This figure is larger, possibly to indicate importance

African carvings of German colonial officials of the early 20th century, Tanzania

COLONIZATION

When Europeans first arrived on the west coast of Africa in the late 1500s, they were interested in trading for gold and slaves. By the end of the 1800s, European nations were not only exploiting the peoples of Africa but also competing with each other for gold, diamonds, copper, and land. They drew boundaries on maps with no regard for the local peoples, such as the Tuareg of the Sahara, the San of the Kalahari Desert, and the cattle herders of eastern Africa. The boundaries completely changed the traditional ways of life of these people, who depend on their ability to travel with herds in search of water.

LIFE IN THE CITIES

As empires grew, so did major cities as centers for trade. In the 1500s, Timbuktu, in the savanna region of northern Africa, was a center of learning, and Gao, capital of the Songhay empire, was home to 75,000 people. Some cities were modernized during colonial rule. For example, Cairo, founded in A.D. 641, expanded rapidly in the 1830s under French rule. As traditional ways of life have changed, many people have migrated to cities, such as Harare in Zimbabwe (left), to find work, but they often retain strong links with their rural "homes."

Mining for gold, Burkina Faso

TROPICAL RAIN FORESTS

There were once tropical rain forests across much of central Africa. Because of poor farming methods and the cutting down of trees for export, the hot, humid rain forests are now found only on the west coast and as far inland as eastern Zaire.

MINERAL RESOURCES

Africa is rich in mineral resources. Some of them – for example, the copper belt of Zaire, the diamond mines of Tanzania, and the gold deposits of South Africa – are exploited on a large scale. Most mineral extraction requires a large labor force and sophisticated machinery and technology.

THE UPLANDS OF AFRICA

Some of the mountains of Africa are so high that the tallest peaks, such as Mount Kilimanjaro on the border of Kenya and Tanzania, are always covered in snow. A layer of cloud causes mists, and water drips onto the dense forests below. Crops are often grown on the fertile high ground—for example, coffee on the slopes of Mount Kilimanjaro and tea in Uganda, Malawi, and Kenya.

A place to live

WHEN YOU TRAVEL around Africa, you see an enormous variety of buildings made from a wide range of materials. The type of dwellings depend not only on what is available locally but also on the lifestyle of the occupants. For example, the San of the Kalahari desert live by traveling through their territory, hunting game and collecting fruits. They carry few possessions and are without means of transportation, so they set up temporary shelters of sticks or branches covered with grass or leaves. Most other groups, such as the millet farmers of Chad in West Africa or the Nupe of Nigeria, need to have permanent dwellings close to their fields. They build their houses, often circular in shape, with a framework of wood, mud walls, and a grass thatched roof. These houses are erected near each other in a compound that has a surrounding wall for defense (see pages 16–17).

These pieces of wood help support the structure and serve as scaffolding during repairs

A PLACE OF WORSHIP
In the savanna regions of Africa, where the Islamic religion holds sway, enormous mosques are built. They are made from mud bricks that have been left in the sun to dry before being built into walls with mud plaster. Mud is an excellent material in hot, dry climates, and can withstand heavy rainfall if dried out by the sun soon afterward.

ON THE MOVE
In drier parts of Africa, such as Somalia, where there are no permanent rivers and little rainfall, the only reliable means of staying alive is to keep herds of animals. Because people have to be constantly on the move in search of water and grazing land, they live a nomadic life and need only temporary shelter. Each married woman has her own house, a collapsible structure of mats over a framework of branches, which she takes apart and packs onto a camel when it it time to move on.

Walls are built from sun-baked mud

A Somali nomadic family outside their collapsible house

HOUSE DECORATION
In parts of southern Africa, women decorate the outside walls of their houses with vivid and bold designs. At first sight, the Ndebele paintings appear to be a series of geometric shapes, but they are, in fact, a representation of architecture. The vertical and horizontal lines represent house supports and beams. The women make the designs with their fingers, hands, or brushes and fabric cloths.

8

Wall surrounding a district

LIVING ON WATER

Building houses on stilts to raise the floor above ground level has many advantages. Houses can be built on mountainous slopes or over water. Air circulates easily and the stilts are a protection from dangerous mammals and snakes. The space beneath houses built on land is often used for storage or to keep domestic cattle. Whole fishing villages, such as this one (right) in Benin, are built on water, and the only access is by dugout canoe.

LIFE ON THE CLIFFS

The Dogon peoples of Mali build their villages in high sandstone cliffs for defense. The villages are divided into districts, each surrounded by a stone wall. The only way into a village is through a narrow doorway, and the only building outside the wall is the men's house.

ANCIENT AND MODERN

The structure of many towns in Morocco reflects the Muslim or European communities that live there. The traditional Muslim town, or medina (left), has an entrance gate. Inside, there are covered markets, ancient mosques, and houses built around hidden courtyards. Later, when the Europeans arrived, they built new towns with wide, tree-lined streets.

Weathering means that mud walls have to be frequently replastered

Great civilizations

Large wooden seeds, covered in gold, are symbols of fertility or wealth

Ceremonial sword from treasure of King Kofi-Karikari (1867–75), Asante, Ghana

Unsharpened iron blade, never intended for war

FROM THE EARLIEST TIMES, the African peoples south of the Sahara Desert lived in scattered family groups and used tools of wood, bone, or stone to fish, hunt wild game, and gather fruit. During the first millenium B.C., there were two great advances in technology that carried these people out of the Stone Age. The first was the organized cultivation of food and the raising of herds, which encouraged people to settle in one place, farm lands, and develop their arts and crafts. The second advance was the production of metal tools and weapons. By A.D. 400, many communities had realized that they had control over metals such as gold and iron ore, and that this gave them power.

STONE AGE ART
Life in Africa depends on an understanding of animals, plants, and the seasons. The earliest peoples recognized their importance and reflected this in superb rock paintings. Not only did they represent themselves but also the animals that they herded or hunted. Most of the early cave paintings show wild animals – elephants, giraffes, rhinoceroses, and ostriches.

THE ASANTE EMPIRE AND ITS GOLD
The Asante peoples of West Africa became the major Gold Coast power of the 18th century, because of their ability to mine, work, and trade in metals. The realization that they could trade profitably with other nations led them to expand their empire along the west coast of Africa, and they became major exporters of slaves to America (pp. 50–51).

THE KUSH CIVILIZATION
The Nubian peoples of Kush lived in what is now known as the Sudan. They rose to power in 800 B.C., establishing an independent kingdom that dominated Egypt and controlled the southern trade routes. They were strong in war, and developed one of the world's earliest alphabetical scripts. The rock-cut temples of Rameses II (1304–1237 B.C.) at Abu Simbel (above) are typical of the widespread monument building of his reign. After 1,000 years, the Kushite civilization declined and finally, in about A.D. 550, was conquered by the neighboring kingdom of Aksum, in today's Ethiopia.

Statue of the sky god, Horus

The tomb owner's wife offers prayers and thanks

ANCIENT EGYPT
From 3000 B.C., the fertile Nile valley was the home of one of the greatest of all civilizations – Egypt, united under the pharaohs. The land was easily irrigated and the Egyptians were able to produce all the food they needed. The Nile River provided an excellent transportation system and trade route for the export of gold and copper from the eastern desert. And it was from Asia, via the Nile River, that Egypt was exposed to concepts such as brick-making and writing.

Hunter (above) and giraffe (left), from prehistoric cave paintings, Matopo Hills, Zimbabwe

The Great Enclosure, Great Zimbabwe, Zimbabwe

Outer wall was 16 ft (5 m) thick at base and 30 ft (9.7 m) high

The bird may be a hawk, vulture, or fish-eagle

Bird is 14 in (0.35 m) tall, and tops a column

GREAT ZIMBABWE

Great Zimbabwe was one of the largest, wealthiest, and most sophisticated of the ancient sub-Saharan cultures. There is evidence that there were people living on the site in prehistoric times. By A.D. 1200, Zimbabwean gold and copper were being mined and exported to Syria and Jordan, as well as to other parts of Asia, in exchange for imported goods, including glass, beads, and Chinese porcelain. The rulers of Zimbabwe developed trading contacts by way of the east coast port of Kilwa, and by 1300, a powerful state had come into being, with Great Zimbabwe as its commercial center. The settlement reached the height of its power in the early 1400s.

Sculptures of the Ife Oni (kings) were always idealized portraits

A unique and mysterious conical tower of solid stone

Parallel lines over whole face are typical of Ife heads

MEMORIALS IN STONE

Soft soapstone rock, found locally, was used to make many objects for the settlement of Great Zimbabwe, including dishes with animal decorations. This soapstone bird is one of only eight that have been found, although there are many plain columns of soapstone, usually positioned on top of outer walls or set in groups on the ground. It is possible that they may have been set there to act as reminders of people who died. Like the conical tower, the possible religious significance of the birds is shrouded in mystery.

THE PEOPLE OF IFE, NIGERIA

In Yoruba legend, the city of Ife was the place where the gods came down to populate the earth. The children of the first god, Odudua, are said to have spread out from Ife, founding their own forest kingdoms in west Africa. The people of Ife certainly influenced much of the art and culture of the neighboring states – a metal-worker is said to have taught the lost-wax process (pp. 54–55) to the people of Benin. Between A.D. 1050 and 1500, the people of Ife produced superb terra cotta and bronze statues of humans and animals. Heads such as this one were used in state funerals.

Bronze head, possibly of an Ife Oni, although it may represent the sea god Olokun

Building a house

PEOPLE BUILD HOUSES for protection from cold, wind, rain, or sun, and use a variety of materials, usually from the local environment. In Africa, there are many people who, having migrated to the cities to find work, live in apartments and townhouses. But there are also many living in rural areas who build traditional houses like this one in Botswana. In that country there are large villages, with the main *kgotla*, or meetinghouse, in the center in the shade of a tree. Most villages have a standpipe for water, a post office, and shops. Building a house like this one is usually done by men and women during the winter months, when the plowing and the harvesting are over. Near the house are smaller shelters for cooking, for brewing beer, and for keeping domestic animals.

Thatch is trimmed at edges with a sharp knife when roof is complete

Roof truss to strengthen roof

Rafters

Posts support roof structure

Walls are plastered both inside and outside in two or three layers

Rafters are tied in position with wire or tree-bark string

BUILDING THE FRAMEWORK
Having marked out the area the house is to occupy, the first stage is for the women to build a circular mud-brick wall. Two types of brick can be used. Wet bricks are shaped by hand, set in place, and covered with plaster. Dried bricks are made in wooden molds, dried in the Sun, and fixed in place with mortar before they too are covered in plaster.

Thatch hangs over house posts

Veranda wall built up to protect the house from rains

STRENGTHENING THE ROOF
The task of collecting the timber and building the roof is undertaken by the men of the village. The first rafters are fixed to the supporting posts outside the wall of the house, and fixed to each other at a central point. Thinner poles or beams are now added and lashed to the first rafters. Sometimes extra support is given by a central vertical pole in the middle of the house.

INTERIOR OF A TUAREG TENT
The lifestyle of the nomadic Tuareg means that they must live in structures that can be taken down and set up easily. The roofs of their tents are made from, on average, 30 or 40 sheep– and goatskins that are tanned and sewn together. The skins are supported on wooden tent poles, and the side walls are made from grass matting.

TYING ON THE THATCH

To thatch a roof, grass or reeds are collected and tied in bundles. The bundles are spread in layers on top of the 16 rafters that form the roof, and fixed in position with tree-bark string or wire. Wooden pegs are placed at the bottom of each rafter to keep the grass bundles from sliding off.

DIFFERENT MATERIALS

Many houses are built with materials that are found locally. These Dinka women in the Sudan are building a house with reeds. The Dinka spend part of the year in permanent villages, and the rest of it in temporary camps.

Reed structure used when Dinkas travel in search of water

Cross-section of wall showing mud bricks

Floors are often decorated with intricate patterns

TAKING A LOOK INSIDE

The floor of the interior is built up after the roof of the house has been completed. A layer of plaster is put on and smoothed with a piece of slate. A mixture of cow dung and water is then made, and a layer put on in which patterns are drawn. In some houses, polished cement plaster covers the floor.

Hunter carrying curved knife

THE FINISHED HOUSE

Women often plaster the walls of houses in Botswana with different-colored clays to give a two-tone effect, darker at the bottom and lighter at the top. The surface of the walls is worn away gradually by rain, and the houses need replastering once or twice a year.

VERANDA POST

Among the Yoruba peoples of Nigeria, the veranda post may not only be a structural support. It can also be an elaborate, decorative carving. This example shows a hunter. Such carvings are found in palaces, shrines, and the houses of chiefs.

Home life

THE PREPARATION and cooking of food, and crafts such as pottery and weaving, are outdoor activities in much of rural Africa. Tents and houses are used for shelter from the rain, to keep warm during cold weather, and for sleeping. The staple diet consists mainly of grains, usually sorghum (a type of wheat), corn, or cassava, with vegetables, such as beans or peas. They are pounded into a soft, sticky pudding to which boiled water or, sometimes, milk is added. A tasty meat or fish stew is cooked separately and eaten with the cooked cereal.

EATING A MEAL
Eating and drinking is a communal activity. Whole families eat together, usually outside. These Tuareg men are heating water to make tea. The Tuareg live in large nomadic groups in the Sahara desert in the south of Algeria. They are Muslims, and the men cover their faces with a veil. They keep goats and sheep as well as camels, and camel milk is their main food.

Hanging milk pot, Somalia

Stopper

Stone pestle and wooden mortar for pounding coffee beans

Skin-covered raffia container for carrying coffeepot

Earthenware coffeepot

Beaded pot rest

TRAVELING COFFEE MACHINE
The Bene-Amer peoples live in Sudan near the border with Eritrea. They are nomadic and travel over a wide area in search of water and pasture for their camels, sheep, and goats. Coffee is an important part of their diet, and they carry coffee-making equipment with them. In other parts of Africa, tea is a favorite beverage, and beer and palm wine are often made by women and sold in markets and beer halls.

OSTRICH EGGSHELL CARRIER
Empty ostrich eggshells, if pierced at one end, make excellent milk or water carriers. The San of the Kalahari Desert use these shells exclusively as water containers, which they store within their territory and use during a drought.

STIRRING IT UP
Wooden food stirrers are often used when cooking grains or stews. These Somali stirrers are typical of the inventive uses to which wood is put. They are rolled between the hands so that the end rotates quickly, much like an electric mixer.

SERVING FOOD
Wooden vessels are used throughout the African continent. They range from a simple, plain style to highly decorated containers that can be used in a king's palace or for ritual purposes. Bowls like this one from Lesotho are traditionally carved from a single block of wood. Wooden containers and calabashes are important among herding communities, because they believe using anything else will cause their cattle to become ill.

SHAPING AND CARVING

The calabash is a gourd that has been grown naturally. When it is ripe, it is soaked in water until the contents have rotted. It is then opened, and the inside cleaned, before it is dried. During the drying process, it becomes hard and can be carved. Although the women often make their own gourds, there are specialists who decorate the surfaces.

Calabash ladle

Scorched pattern is etched with hot metal point

FOOD IN THE WILD

Among the hunter-gatherers such as the San of southern Africa, the men are mainly responsible for hunting, and the women for collecting berries. If, during their search, the women find a tree full of berries, and there is a watering hole nearby, the group will stay in the area for some time. They build temporary shelters, one for each family, from branches and grass, set against supporting trees.

SMOKING FOR PLEASURE

Pipe-smoking is a popular relaxation enjoyed by both men and women in Africa. Hemp was traditionally smoked in water pipes of animal horn or calabashes by people all over Africa. It was inhaled through a mouthful of water to control its powerful effect on the smoker. The introduction of tobacco led to the making of wooden and clay pipes. Many were decorated with elaborate and intricate designs, like these Xhosa pipes from the Transkei region of South Africa.

Pot is hung from the roof by a rope net

Incised metal decoration

Village bread oven made of clay

STORING PLACE

A variety of containers are found inside a house, on shelves or suspended on ropes for protection against rats, mice, and snakes. Precious possessions are often hidden in the roof. A porous clay pot like this one will keep water cool, and acts as a short-term refrigerator. Pots are usually made by the women, although, in some parts of Africa, pottery is exclusively produced by the men of a village.

BAKING DAY

Grains such as cassava, corn, and sorghum can be ground into flour. Water is added, and the flour paste flattened into circular shapes and baked. Here, a family in Timbuktu, Mali, waits to eat the freshly cooked bread.

Life in the compound

IN MANY PARTS OF AFRICA, family groups live in compounds that are often circular in shape. They are made up of several clay houses with thatched roofs, connected by passageways. There is a meeting place in the center of the compound, an enclosure for the householder, and an area for each of his wives. Each enclosure has a sleeping house, containing personal belongings, a kitchen, a granary, and a storage house, which is used for agricultural tools, domestic utensils, dried food, and milk. This homestead of the Kuanyama people in Angola was home to a farming family in the 1930s, and was probably occupied for about ten years. The family would then build a new homestead nearby, reusing materials where possible.

A WOMAN'S WORK
Within a family group, men and women usually have separate tasks. The women look after their children, work in the fields, fish, and prepare food. This woman, in a Habila settlement in the Sudan, is grinding beans before cooking them. Women also fetch and carry water and firewood, as well as looking after their own area of the compound. In many family groups, such as the Kuanyama, the women make pottery for use in the home.

DAILY LIFE IN THE COMPOUND
The agricultural life of the Kuanyama is based on the seasons. The compound is built, following a traditional plan, near a permanent waterhole. The grainfields where the Kuanyama grow their staple foods – millet and sorghum – surround the compound, and there are rainy season and dry pens for the cattle. The wealth of a particular householder is measured by the number of wives he has and by the quality of his compound and herds.

This householder has two granaries

Guest house

Rainy season cattle pens

Householder's enclosure

Cattle moved here because they do not need to be close to waterhole

Fence of hewn stakes 10 ft (3m) high

Enclosure for pounding harvested millet and sorghum

Sleeping hut

The householder's granaries were always bigger than those of his wives

CATTLE HERDING
In the drier regions of Africa, cattle are kept as the main source of food and the men look after them. The cattle are used for the meat, milk, and clothing – the skins are tanned and made into leather clothes and shoes. Because some communities rely on natural grazing land, they have to move from area to area to exploit seasonal weather changes and to find water. They build temporary camps at each place. These cattle belong to one such community in the Sudan.

Model of a Kuanyama people's homestead, Angola, West Africa, made in the 1930s by the people who lived there

Cattle pen close to the waterhole in the dry season

STORING GRAIN
For thousands of years, storage houses and granaries in Africa have been associated with a householder's status. The more granaries he has, the richer and more influential he is. Large storage containers are raised off the ground to protect against infestation by rats and mice.

Pen for calves

Chicken roost

Dairy

First wife's enclosure

Central enclosure or meeting place

Storage hut with wooden shelves

Sleeping hut with bed

Second wife's enclosure, with roofs of buildings removed

Goat pen

Smaller granary of second wife

Indoor kitchen with open fire

Network of passageways running all the way around outer fence of compound

House used by children of the compound during the day

MAKING MEALIE MEAL
A young girl rhythmically pounds mealie meal (finely ground corn) in a compound in Zimbabwe. Like the shelters in the Kuanyama compound, the houses here are circular, made of clay, and have thatched roofs. The girl is using a wooden mortar and stone pestle, and she grinds the meal into fine grains. She will then add boiled water to make the porridge that is her family's staple food. In the dry season, preparation of food will take place in the open air. However, in many compounds, there is an indoor kitchen that is used by everyone during the rainy season.

Finding food

MOST OF AFRICA'S RURAL population farms the land or keeps livestock such as cattle or sheep, despite problems caused by drought or soil erosion. However, there are also small populations who live almost entirely by finding wild foods. Of these, there are three main groups: the San of Namibia and Botswana, the Hadza of Tanzania, and the pygmies of Zaire. These groups are called hunter-gatherers – in other words, they traditionally hunt game animals and birds, and gather insects, roots, fruits, and wild honey. They do not live in permanent villages, but in small nomadic groups that may camp together for part of the year. Hunting is done by the men, and gathering by the women. Surprisingly, their way of life is often easier than that of the farmers.

MARKET DAYS
Most of the food that the farmers grow, as well as many of the animals that are herded, are taken to be sold at a local market. Women are often the traders in markets, such as this colorful one near Nairobi, in Kenya.

FOR THE BIRDS
This bird trap was used by a Dinka herdsboy in the Sudan to catch birds. It was hung between the branches of a tree. Birds, unable to see its fine lines – made from giraffe hair and weighted with clay – would become ensnared in it.

CATCHING ANTELOPE
The Turkana people of Kenya use this wooden trap to catch antelope. They leave it lying on the ground and simply wait until the animal puts its foot in the hole.

Once in the snare, the antelope cannot withdraw its foot

FARMING THE FIELDS
In many areas of Africa, most of the work of raising crops is still done with the hoe and by hand. This laborious work is often carried out by women, while the men look after the livestock. In some communities, the men farm for their prospective in-laws as part of the marriage agreement. Many of the women, like this one in Sierra Leone, work in the fields all day with their babies on their backs.

Stone spindle

Wooden spindle

FISHING FOR A LIVING
Fishermen use nets, baskets, hooks, lines, traps, and dams in shallow waters to catch fish for a living. They sell the fish to women, who then cure them and, in turn, sell them at the markets. This dugout canoe is particularly narrow because it is used to weave in and out of the roots of mangroves in the coastal waters of West Africa. When not in use, the canoe is turned bottom-up and raised several feet off the ground on a light trestle table. This helps it to dry out and keeps the wood from rotting.

The hide noose is tied around a tree so the animal cannot escape

SPINNING A TRAP
These spindles carry fishing lines of cotton thread that the Bagiun peoples of Ciula Island in Somalia use to catch fish for their daily diet. The baited lines are trailed in the water from fishing boats. Traditionally, Africans catch fish to eat, or to dry and sell. Fishing purely for sport is unknown.

Dugout canoe, West Africa

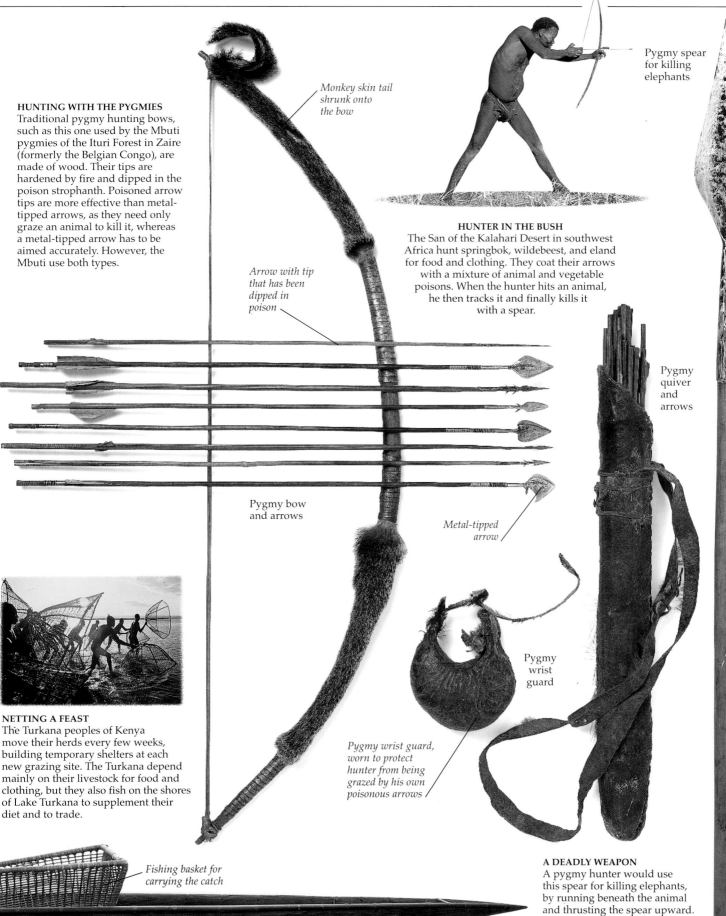

HUNTING WITH THE PYGMIES

Traditional pygmy hunting bows, such as this one used by the Mbuti pygmies of the Ituri Forest in Zaire (formerly the Belgian Congo), are made of wood. Their tips are hardened by fire and dipped in the poison strophanth. Poisoned arrow tips are more effective than metal-tipped arrows, as they need only graze an animal to kill it, whereas a metal-tipped arrow has to be aimed accurately. However, the Mbuti use both types.

Monkey skin tail shrunk onto the bow

Pygmy spear for killing elephants

HUNTER IN THE BUSH

The San of the Kalahari Desert in southwest Africa hunt springbok, wildebeest, and eland for food and clothing. They coat their arrows with a mixture of animal and vegetable poisons. When the hunter hits an animal, he then tracks it and finally kills it with a spear.

Arrow with tip that has been dipped in poison

Pygmy quiver and arrows

Pygmy bow and arrows

Metal-tipped arrow

Pygmy wrist guard

Pygmy wrist guard, worn to protect hunter from being grazed by his own poisonous arrows

NETTING A FEAST

The Turkana peoples of Kenya move their herds every few weeks, building temporary shelters at each new grazing site. The Turkana depend mainly on their livestock for food and clothing, but they also fish on the shores of Lake Turkana to supplement their diet and to trade.

Fishing basket for carrying the catch

A DEADLY WEAPON

A pygmy hunter would use this spear for killing elephants, by running beneath the animal and thrusting the spear upward. The wound did not usually kill the elephant immediately, but would do so within 24 hours, during which time the hunter would track the animal.

Pattern and color

IN AFRICA, pattern and color are important ingredients of everyday life. Materials, pots, and baskets are often covered in geometric, animal, human, or floral shapes. Certain objects, such as pots and calabashes, are made by people for their own use; others, such as textiles, are made by specialists who make a living from their skills. Local resources offer an excellent source of materials from which to make and decorate the objects. The forests provide wood from which stools and figures are carved, and bark that is beaten into a versatile cloth, while seeds and vegetable dyes are used for decoration. Many objects are made for religious purposes or for kings or rulers. These are usually highly decorated.

Gourd is burnished with a hot knife

CARVING AND DECORATING GOURDS
Gourds grow in most parts of Africa. When cut and dried they are used as food bowls, serving dishes, and sound boxes for musical instruments (pp. 60-61). The natural color of a gourd is yellow, but it can be dyed with plant dyes. Carvers often cut a series of geometric shapes into the gourd (left) before it is dyed.

DYE PITS
Many materials can be colored with natural dyes, often made by pounding plants and mixing them with water or another substance. For example, the crushed leaves of the plant *Lonchocarpus cyanescens* produce the blue dye indigo when mixed with the ash of green wood. Often fabrics or leather are dyed in vats set into the ground, as they are here in Marrakesh in Morocco.

Bark

Beater made from ivory and wood

Barkcloth can be used for clothing or for sleeping mats

Warthog-tusk beater with wooden handle

CLOTH MADE FROM TREES
Trees are a ready source of materials, for both objects and dyes. In Uganda, a special fabric is produced from them. The bark is stripped off the trees, which are then covered with banana leaves for protection. The bark is softened by soaking in water, or by steaming in a bundle over a fire. It is then placed on a wooden log, a piece at a time, and beaten with a heavy mallet. The frequent beating of the bark causes its fibers to knit together to become cloth.

RAFFIA CLOTHS
In many parts of Africa, raffia, the grasslike fiber of the raffia palm, is used to make a wide variety of everyday things such as ropes, fishing tackle, and snares for catching wild animals. Young leaves are stripped and peeled, carefully dried in the sun, and mounted on a loom to be woven into cloth. Usually a loom is kept inside a weaver's house, but some are outside in the village, under a shelter for shade in the hot sun.

MAKING A MAT, SOMALIA
Many mats and baskets are woven from vegetable fibers, usually by women in the home. Little equipment is needed – just a knife to split the strands of fiber. It is an activity that is popular with many cattle herders and hunter-gatherers who are constantly on the move, as well as settled farming groups.

WEAVING ON A LOOM
Both men and women weave cloth on looms. Two sets of fibers or threads are used to make the cloth: the first set, warp threads, are arranged horizontally or vertically. Above, the warp threads are wound around the poles in the ground. The second set, weft threads, are passed in and out between the warp threads to form the fabric. The cloth varies in width according to the loom.

CUT-PILE CLOTHS, ZAIRE
The Kuba peoples of Zaire produce a highly distinctive embroidered cloth (above) using a technique known as "cut-pile." The base cloth is a piece of woven raffia. The raffia embroidery thread is threaded on a needle, which is used to pick up a few threads of the base cloth, before pulling the embroidery thread underneath. The embroidery thread is cut, leaving its two ends visible as a pattern on the surface of the base cloth. Pieces of embroidered cloth are sewn together to form one large piece of fabric. The pattern is created from memory, and the same patterns are found on carved objects and houses.

MULTI-COLORED CLOTHS, MADAGASCAR
In 19th-century Madagascar, cotton, silk, and raffia were woven into colorful shawls that were worn by both men and women over European clothing. Local vegetable dyes were traditionally used to produce the colors of the textiles, but the introduction of manufactured dyes increased the range still further. The designs are so complicated that the weaver often uses bits of numbered paper to figure out at which point the pattern is to be formed.

The edge is typically frayed to form a fringe

The colors and patterns in cloths from Madagascar combine vividly

Sports and entertainment

WHEN THE DAILY WORK IS OVER, African peoples relax in various ways. Storytelling is a favorite occupation, and lives of important ancestors are often reenacted around the communal fire in the compound. Music can be performed either by an individual playing a lute or harp or by a group. Music is also played as part of village competitions, which include other activities, such as wrestling, racing, and dance. Among the Mursi peoples of Ethiopia, fierce dueling contests with long poles are organized by young unmarried men. The Acholi of Uganda play a game called undile that is similar to hockey. The board game, mancala, has often been called the national game of Africa, and is played everywhere.

FULANI DANCE TROUPE
The Fulani of West Africa have a strong tradition of singing, storytelling, and dancing. These talents are highly regarded. Groups of "street" musicians called griots perform in the open air.

Musicians carved on wooden door lintel, Ibibio, Nigeria

NUBA WRESTLING GAMES
In many places, young men enjoy wrestling. Huge crowds gather for village competitions among the Nuba of the Sudan. The men are judged for their strength and skill by a referee. The wrestlers are fiercely competitive, and the wrestling champion earns himself a special position in the community.

GAMES OF WAR
In some societies, where strength and skill in fighting is important, young boys are encouraged to play games to prepare for their later lives as warriors. Zulu boys, for example, use fighting sticks in a game similar to fencing, becoming expert at striking and avoiding blows.

Painted pebbles used as playing pieces

Players lift the pebbles and redistribute them counterclockwise

Toy gun copied from a European firearm, Azande, Sudan

Somali doll made from corn husk and cloth

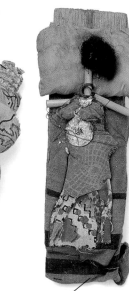

Doll in bed, part of a complete doll's house, from Cameroon

Cameroon doll made from wood and feathers

Cameroon portrait of a European woman

HOMEMADE TOYS
African children are ingenious at making their own toys from scrap materials. Toys made from wire – cars, helicopters, and trucks – are quite common. This boy has made a car from heavy wire, using shoe-polish cans for the wheels.

Statues carved on a lintel, probably from a shrine or secret society house

Ostriches can run at 30 mph (48 kph)

DOLLS WITH A PURPOSE
Although many dolls are made simply for the amusement of children, some play a crucial role in the life of young girls. The *akua'ba* dolls of the Asante, for example, are made because it is believed they guarantee the owner will have children in the future. Some dolls are made for ceremonies, such as the initiation of young girls into womanhood. A variety of different materials, such as wood, beads, wax, and nails, are used to emphasize different features of some of these dolls.

OSTRICH RACING, SOUTH AFRICA
Camel, horse, and ostrich racing are popular spectator sports in parts of Africa. Berber horsemen ride to display their skills on special occasions, and the Tuareg peoples of the Sahara often race camels.

When pieces are moved from one cup to another, it is called "sowing"

MUSIC AND MUSICIANS
Music is a part of everyday life, and Africans produce a variety of instruments from available materials (pp. 60–61). Music is played as a background to events such as sports or wrestling. It is also an integral part of social occasions such as ceremonies, masquerades (pp. 62–63), or religious rites. Kings and chiefs often have musicians at their courts to sing praises in their honor.

Leather pouch to hold mancala pieces

PLAYING THE GAME
Mancala is found everywhere, and, as well as being played on carved boards, is often simply scratched on rock or in the sand.

THE GAME OF MANCALA
Mancala is a board game for two or more players that is played all over Africa. The wooden mancala board consists of two rows of holes, and the playing pieces are usually pebbles, although seeds, beans, cowrie shells, peas, and even buttons can be used. The object is to win all your opponent's playing pieces, but the rules of the game and the number of players varies according to region.

Wooden mancala board, Maasai, Kenya

Female dress

WEARING A BABY
African mothers often carry their babies on their backs, tied on with a shawl or a piece of fabric. This method of carrying babies has influenced the design of baby slings used by European and American women, as it is an efficient way of caring for a child while doing other tasks.

P EOPLE WEAR CLOTHES for a variety of reasons other than to keep warm, or as a protection from the sun or rain. Clothes are worn for modesty, or to advertise age, position in society, wealth, or occupation. Often, people have different or more showy clothes for important ceremonies or rituals ceremonies. Among the Maasai, the women wear skirts of animal hide and numerous beaded ornaments for different occasions. However, only the married women wear brass earrings, which indicates their status in society.

Second wig of braided hair is made and worn at end of ceremonies

Topknot

Second wig

Veil

Beard

MARRIAGE WEAR
For the Kuanyama peoples of Angola, the initiation and engagement ceremonies for young girls were combined into one event lasting several days. Each girl was given a special wig with shell decorations, and wore a hide skirt, apron, and beads. During the event, this first wig was ceremoniously burned, and a second wig, topknot, and beard were given to her. The girls wore the beards in imitation of men. They were then ready for the transition into womanhood.

Dress is made of printed cotton

Wide-elbowed sleeves

Dresses are made with a patchwork of colors

THE CHANGING FACE OF FASHION
The traditional dress of the women of the Herero cattle herders of Namibia was leather aprons, headdress, and elaborate beaded ornamentation. This was abandoned during the 19th century when those Herero who became Christian adopted the dress of the German missionaries. The distinctive, colorful Victorian costume (left) consists of a long dress with a wide stiff skirt, a fitted bodice worn with a shawl, and a "duk" – a cloth wrapped around the head (above).

Victorian-style Herero dress, Namibia

The way the cloth is tied varies from group to group

Cowrie shells sewn on as decoration

Leather cloak and skirt, Karamojong, Uganda

Cloth is printed with geometric and floral patterns

Leather decorated with strings of glass beads

DRESSING TO SHOW STATUS

In most societies, those who possess power and wealth reveal it in their clothing. Especially rare materials are favored by royalty and often costly fabrics are reserved for those of high rank. This queen of Dahomey (above) is wearing elaborate and richly decorated clothes.

Back apron

Front apron

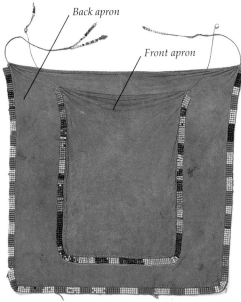

MARRIED STATUS

Among many of the cattle-herding communities of eastern Africa, the clothing a woman wears indicates whether or not she is married. An unmarried girl of the Karamojong, for example, wears a hip skirt and head ornaments. Once married, she may wear a leather cloak and a skirt that is tied at the front. Elaborate skirts are worn on special occasions.

TRADITIONAL APRONS

These traditional front and back aprons are made of tanned leather. Leather is used for a wide variety of items, including clothing, footwear, and shields. Once taken from the carcass of an animal, the hide is quickly cleaned and pegged to the ground to dry in the sun. After a few days, animal fat is rubbed in to soften the leather.

WRAPPED UP

In many parts of western Africa, a married woman wears a large and elaborate head-tie, usually of the same material as her dress. The head-tie is a single piece of fabric that she folds and wraps according to her social group, status, and fashion. Usually, the greater the height and size of the headdress, the more important she is.

Male attire

DIFFERENT CLOTHES CAN INDICATE the many cultural groups to which people belong. They can also give clues about the kind of work a person does, or his or her position in society. In Africa what people wear can show if they live in a desert or forest region, if they are farmers or kings, if it is a hot or cold time of year. Today, many Africans wear western dress, but some types of traditional clothing are making a comeback. Asante kente cloth, which was formerly worn exclusively by royalty and chiefs, is now worn by others. People even wear a combination of western and traditional dress.

Number of feathers increase with seniority of wearer

Ostrich feathers stuck into headress on special occasions

Desert veil, Sudan

CEREMONIAL HEADDRESS
The men of the Karamojong of Uganda wear distinctive and elaborate headdresses of human hair. This headdress was made with hair that had been cut off. Nowadays, a hairdresser gathers the hair on a person's head into a tight bun. It is then covered in clay and painted it with pigments. The whole process can take three days.

The headdress is in the shape of a cow, an important Karamojong symbol

HEADGEAR
Hats are worn by many people in Africa, and the style varies considerably. Sometimes, to protect themselves against the elements, men wear veils – pieces of cloth that can be wrapped around the head and over the face. In western Africa, many men have short hair and frequently wear small caps to match their clothes.

Man wearing beaded hat, Nigeria

The style and color of the beadwork often indicates from what region the man comes

Zulu belt

SIMPLE DRESS
Appearance is very important to the Maasai. The men frequently cover their bodies in red ocher and braid their hair in ocher-colored braids. Because of the emphasis on this aspect of physical appearance, they wear only simple cotton cloth tied at the shoulder.

INFLUENCES FROM THE EAST
During the 19th century, cloth that imitated Javanese dyed material was printed in Amsterdam, in the Netherlands, and in Manchester, England, using a technique in which designs were put on the cloth in stages. The cloth was exported in large quantities to West Africa. This trade still continues, though factories in several West African countries, including Ghana (above), produce the cloth.

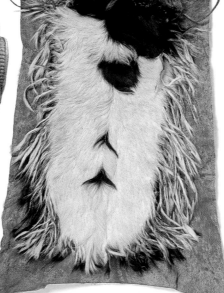

CHANGING CLOTHES AND CUSTOMS
This is a traditional Zulu goatskin front apron that is tied with a beaded belt. The back piece was usually made from oxhide. The aprons form part of the costume that is worn at ceremonies and on special occasions. Traditionally, the Zulu peoples of southern Africa are cattle herders who have retained many of their traditional customs in spite of upheavals caused by western culture. A young man courting a girl will wear western clothes bought in the city as well as the traditional red-and-white courting cloth.

Wooden sandals,
Somalia

Tooled leather
sandals, Uganda

*This beaded crown
portrays a royal ancestor*

*Cross decoration is the **dagi**
knot, an Islamic motif found
in many parts of West Africa*

EXCLUSIVE WEAR
Only kings are allowed to wear beaded
crowns in Yoruba society in Nigeria.
This is because they are believed to be
descendants of Odudua, the mythical
founder and first king of the Yoruba
peoples. The king wears the crown that
is appropriate to a particular ceremony.

FEET AND FOOTWEAR
A variety of materials are used to
make sandals and shoes. Wood
sandals and clogs protect feet from
hot sand and spiky plants, while
leather shoes provide protection
from all weather. Berber women in
Morocco weave not only clothing,
carpets, and tent hangings but also
boots that are worn by both men
and women. The sole is leather, but
the calf-length upper boot is woven
in thick, colorful wool.

*Leather is shaped
by being heated*

Leather sandals,
Somalia

NIGERIAN TUNIC
Yoruba men wear two
types of costumes. One
has a long, loose gown,
and the other a shorter,
knee-length top (right).
Both are worn over
trousers. The outfits are
usually made of local
cloth that has been
woven in narrow
strips, which are then
sewn together. The
neck, the front of the
top, and the bottom
edge of the trousers
are usually embroidered.
A cap of the same fabric is
often worn as well.

Embroidered
boots, Morocco

*Embroidery is
done by men*

DRESSED FOR THE DESERT
People who live in the desert regions of
Africa, such as this man from Algeria, wear
loose clothes to keep cool. The men wear baggy
trousers and long cotton tops. A piece of cloth, or
veil, wrapped around the head, with a narrow gap
for the eyes, is an effective protection against the
sun, heat, and windblown sand of the desert.

Self-adornment

Dinka finger ring made from a pangolin scale

THE WAYS THAT African men and women make themselves attractive is colorful and varied. In some cultures, the size and shape of the body is emphasized – young girls in southeastern Nigeria spend part of their initiation in a "fattening house." In other cultures, particular features are given attention – in Kenya, Kikuyu women wear earlobe plugs because distended earlobes are admired by their men. Colorful dyes are painted directly onto the body of both men and women, or small cuts are made with a knife to form patterns on the skin. These designs often indicate the identity, wealth, and status of a person.

BAUBLES, BANGLES...
Copper wire jewelry is found in many parts of eastern and southern Africa. The items vary from lightweight coiled bangles to heavy copper armlets that can weigh up to 30 lbs (13.5 kg). Copper bracelets, armlets, and anklets are usually worn by women. They often indicate wealth.

Carved hairpins

Pegs for stiffening braided hair

HAIR AND HAIRPINS
Both men and women spend a lot of time decorating their hair, sometimes into elaborate styles. Hairpins are often used, both for practical reasons and, in the case of the carved pins, as decoration. Oil is often used on the hair, since its shine indicates health.

...AND BEADS
Today, South African women wear ornate beaded necklaces, cloaks, and headgear and produce beaded items to sell to tourists. The traditional thread used for stringing beads imported from Europe was a fine gut that was strong and durable. By twisting this between the fingers, a point was made to put through the beads. Nowadays, a needle and thread are used.

Wooden hairpins

HENNA HANDS
In many parts of northern and western Africa, henna dye is used to paint intricate patterns on the hands, feet, and face. Although it is used by men and children, it is more commonly applied by women, not only to make themselves beautiful but also to protect them against evil.

White beads indicate love

Pink usually indicates "bride price", given by the groom to the bride's family

Ropes of beads are worn as girdles and belts

Zulu beaded necklet, South Africa

A FORM OF COMMUNICATION
Beads are worn by men and women around the head, neck, waist, and arms. They are worn as decoration and as a form of communication. Young Zulu girls in South Africa make beaded necklets (center left) for their boyfriends, called "love letters." The pattern and color of the Zulu beads carry different meanings. For example, white is associated with purity and truth, red can mean anger and pain, and blue can refer to being faithful.

Comb is held in the middle to tease out hair from the scalp in styling

Belt worn by a man

Dinka belt, Sudan

Red is associated with blood, sexuality, and fire

Hair is dressed with earth, butter, and fibers to show vitality

After marriage, Maasai women wear more beaded collars to signal a different status

COMBING IT OUT
Wooden combs of all shapes and sizes are used to shape and style the hair. Some, such as the one above right, can also be worn as decoration.

Today, plastic beads are often used instead of glass

GETTING THE MESSAGE
Among the Samburu and the Maasai of Kenya, young, single men are very colorful and eager to attract attention. They gather to boast and dance in front of young girls. The young Samburu male (above) pays a great deal of attention to his personal appearance, painting his body with red ocher and wearing an array of beads. The number of beaded necklaces worn by a Maasai woman (right) indicates whether she is married, if she has children, and how wealthy she is.

29

Rulers and leaders

THERE WERE THREE MAIN methods of government in traditional Africa. The first, found in the ancient empires such as Mali and Songhay, consisted of loosely connected states where individual emirs held sway locally. By contrast, the then forest kingdoms of western and central Africa – Ghana, Benin, and Dahomey – were ruled by all-powerful kings who had a complex hierarchy of officials under them. The third type was mainly found in eastern Africa, where groups such as the Maasai democratically elected councils of elders.

EMPIRES OF THE SAVANNA
By the 15th century, Africa had a number of states, kingdoms, and empires, such as Mali and Songhay, that were based on trade and warfare. Their rulers (above and above right) were depicted by 16th-century Portuguese mapmakers.

Carved elephant tusk, Benin city

Tusks were carved with stories of myth and legend

These tusks were slotted into the top of memorial heads (below right)

Neck rings in imitation of coral bead collar only worn by an Oba

KEEPING COOL
Flywhisks were always a practical solution to keeping cool and swatting the flies that irritated. However, they have also become symbols of authority for appearances in public by people in authority. Whisks with highly decorated handles were usually owned by chiefs.

Flywhisk made of cow's hair

IN MEMORIAM
Kings had absolute power, and combined religious and state authority. The accession to kingship was generally celebrated by the king performing certain rites that set him apart from ordinary people. In recognition of this, the peoples of the Benin cast brass memorial heads of their Obas, or kings, and placed them in a special shrine at which sacrifices were made.

Wooden handle

Umbrellas often topped with gold images of crescents, birds, and weapons

DECORATIVE STATUS SYMBOLS
The Asantehene, king of the Asante peoples of Ghana, always appears under an enormous multicolored umbrella with a hanging border, a symbol of a chief's presence. A guild of specialists make elaborate umbrellas for the king and his senior chiefs. When the king walks along, his umbrella bearer twirls the umbrella around in time to music and sings the king's praises.

Probably the representation of a king

Rifle as second symbol of status

Queen Nzinga used her servant as a stool because she was not offered a chair by a Portuguese official

Swagger sticks, Umbundu, Angola

Knife as first symbol of status

Yoruba crowns were believed to contain all the knowledge of generations of kings

A ROYAL AUDIENCE
The female relatives of the king – his wives, "mothers", and sisters – often represented him. Above, Queen Nzinga of Natamba, Angola, meets Portuguese traders. It was important that a royal person should be seated, or offered a seat, during any discussion. The king of the Kuba peoples of Zaire also, on occasion, used a courtier as a stool.

SWAGGER STICKS
One of these swagger sticks (right), probably based on the European walking stick, was carried at all times by a chief of the Ovimbundu of Angola. The Ovimbundu were great traders of southern Africa in the 19th century. They had a king but were, in effect, governed by his relatives or ministers through a system of chiefdoms.

COUNCIL OF ELDERS
In some smaller communities, a group of democratically elected elders are responsible for making decisions. They meet informally to discuss problems and to seek everyone's agreement on the solutions. Here (above), a council of elders of the Barbera of Somalia are discussing how to deal with the problem of famine.

The face is probably that of a royal ancestral deity

BEADED CROWNS
The Yoruba kings of Nigeria are believed to be descendants of Odudua, the first king of the Yoruba peoples, and are permitted to wear beaded crowns. Other important figures such as priests and medicine men, who communicate with the spirit world, are also able to wear them, but only the king is able to wear and use beaded accessories such as flywhisks, staffs, and footrests. Some crowns have a long beaded fringe that hides the wearer's face. This helps emphasize his ritual existence as king.

Religion and beliefs

THE MOST WIDESPREAD systems of belief in Africa are the world religions of Christianity and Islam. However, there are many different traditional religions as well, including the belief in many gods and the worship of ancestors. Ancestors are the providers of rules of conduct for a community. If angered, their spirits can inflict harm and must be appeased with offerings. The belief that kings are gods is another important part of traditional religion. The kings of Benin and Ghana, for example, are too holy to speak directly to their subjects and must use a spokesman.

Priest's costume, Nkimba Society, Congo

Carved and painted wooden mask

A LIFETIME OF TRAINING
Sometimes children are identified as future priests and undergo a long training with established masters who teach a wide range of knowledge in great secrecy. The priest is the only person in the community to perform rituals, and he wears a distinctive costume. Each priest owns his mask, which both hides and reveals violent and benevolent powers.

MASKS AND ANCESTORS
Families honor ancestors during annual festivals, and through song, dance, and music, tell of the family's history. A number of masks, such as this Epa mask (right), are paraded in sequence as the story is dramatized.

THE ROLE OF THE PRIEST
The priest is a religious specialist whose job is to maintain, celebrate, and, if necessary, restore the right relationship between the community and the gods. He is an important person, and is concerned with both the physical and the spiritual well-being of his community. People often seek his medical advice, as well as consulting him about social and moral problems.

Feathers attached to woven grass net

Battle gowns were usually made of heavy cotton fabric

Leather pouch containing Koranic script

These smocks are also worn by chiefs at their investment and at funerals

CHARM GOWNS
Islam is a religion that has only one god, Allah, and it is based on the teaching of the Prophet Mohammed, who was born 1,400 years ago in Arabia. Islam is widespread in many parts of Africa, and has affected some traditional religions. This Asante gown (above) is covered in leather pouches that contain sayings from the Islamic holy book, the Koran. These Koranic scripts were believed by the Asante to protect senior warriors during battles.

A BLACK CHRIST
Where people were converted to Christianity, European crucifixes and carvings were copied and gradually took on an African appearance. Figures of St. Anthony, the patron saint of Portugal, were made in large numbers, and often used as healing charms. More recently, some wall paintings, like this one in Mozambique, depict a black Christ.

CHRISTIAN COUNTRIES
Christianity has become the major religion in some African countries. Ethiopia has been Christian since the 4th century A.D., and the priest is highly regarded there. Only the emperor holds a higher position in society, because he is closer to God. Every church in Ethiopia has a completely enclosed inner room, which is entered only by the priest. People gather to worship patron saints and take mass in church on religious and national holidays.

A MISSIONARY ZEAL
Europeans began to establish Christian missions in West Africa from the early 19th century. African traditional values such as the belief in many gods and ancestor figures, were greatly affected. The European missionaries, traders, and officials were frequently represented by African carvers, usually on horseback or wearing a hat to distinguish them from Africans. This one was carved by a Yoruba craftsman in Nigeria.

Continued on next page

Continued from previous page

Rites and rituals

To preserve good health and prosperity, many Africans perform rituals, including ancestor worship. Ancestors are called upon to solve problems, combat evil spirits, cure sickness, and help people through important events in their lives. The priest, who is also the community's healer, contacts the ancestors in various ways. He may go into a trance or use magical objects such as oracle boards or carved figures. The Yoruba of Nigeria and the Dogon of Mali, for example, use an oracle bowl and board. In this way, the priest "divines,"or finds out, what the individual consulting him must do.

DIVINING STAFFS AND THEIR USE
In Africa, there is a belief in the close link between events and the behavior of individuals. Sometimes, the priest uses a divination staff to seek out harmful people. The entire community gathers together as the priest moves the staff around until it points at the person believed to be responsible for the evil.

POWER FIGURES
The belief that invisible forces can be destructive is widespread in Africa. Carved human or animal figures are sometimes made that contain "healing" and "protective" substances, which are placed inside the sculpture or rubbed into it. They are often placed in a container that is at the center of the figure.This process is accompanied by chanting and prayers. These figures can be owned by an entire community or by an individual.

Power figure, Zaire

Magical container at centre of figure

People drive in nails and then pull them out again to release the spirit's power

Divination bowls are often elaborately carved

Divination vessel, Cameroon

DIVINING CEREMONIES
Divination is carried out in many African countries, and one of the most important pieces of equipment is the divination vessel, in which kola nuts are stored. For the Yoruba, the priest performs the rite to solve problems and to establish dates for festivals to honor ancestors and gods. As well as the vessel, he uses a tray which he dusts with flour or powdered wood and on which he marks a pattern. Finally, he has a small tapper, with which he calls upon the god of moral order, Orunmila.

DOGON DIVINATION
The Dogon priest, like the Yoruba priest, uses 16 kola nuts and a tray. He makes a pattern of marks in the dust on the tray to record the number of nuts left behind after he has passed them quickly from one hand to the other several times. The final pattern is the key to a sacred poem recited to the client, who then interprets it for his own purposes.

Divination staff, Mozambique

*Distinctive
curled hairstyle*

*Black dye obtained
from plants or tree
bark and believed
to be powerful*

*These figures
were often worn
around the neck*

*Matching
elaborate
hairdo at
back of head*

CURING ILLNESSES

People believe that illnesses such as headaches, nightmares, and chest pains can be cured by a priest. His medicine pack is frequently placed in the stomach of a smaller carved figure, like this one (above) from Zaire. Sometimes the medicine is covered by a mirror that is believed to warn the owner from which direction harmful threats may come.

*Teeth individually cut
and inserted one by one*

WARDING OFF EVIL SPIRITS

In certain parts of western Africa, carved heads and masks that represent female and male spirits are used in rituals and ceremonies. The female masks are usually of beautiful, serene spirits and have distinctive faces and elaborate hairstyles that are painted black. Other masks are depicted as fierce, terrifying characters, and are usually male. Some of the masks and heads are used in masquerade (pp. 62–63) by the secret societies. For example, the Ekpo secret society of the Ibibio uses carved heads in masquerade. This Bambuku head (right) would have been left in a small shelter at the entrance to a village to scare off evil spirits.

*Typically elaborate
hornlike carving*

*Fierce expression
on this carved
head to scare
away evil spirits*

Carved wooden head
of the Bambuku people
of the Cross River area of
Nigeria and Cameroon

Myth and magic

Stories about the way the world began and how people came into being are often told in Africa. Important or royal ancestors play a central role in these "creation myths," which tell how the ancestors traveled far and wide, fought monsters, invented incredible devices, and established the community. Some of these mythical heroes are also gods who demand regular worship and sacrifice. The stories form part of the initiation into adulthood of young boys and girls, who may also become members of secret societies. The societies play a very important role in decision-making in a community and affect how the community is organized. Each secret society has knowledge that is only available to its members.

LUCKY CHARMS
Certain cultures have been greatly affected by Christianity and Islam, yet still retain some of their traditional religious values. The Galla people of Ethiopia often use cattle charms (above) to ensure successful breeding.

KISSI FIGURE
Carved soapstone figures are thought to be part of the earlier cultures of the Kissi and Mende peoples of Sierra Leone. They are worshipped in shrines as protectors of the harvest.

Neck rings show status of individual

Mende figure is carved from wood

GOOD LUCK CHARMS
Magical charms were often worn for good luck and protection. Soldiers, for example, carried and wore various talismans as a protection against weapons or poison. When going on a journey, a charm made by the local priest may be given to the traveler to protect him or her against any dangers. This traveler's charm is a bundle of torn rags hanging from a carved antelope horn, and would have been carried at all times on the journey.

Figures are associated with healing

SOCIETY FIGURES
These figures are used by women diviners of the Yassi society of the Mende people of Sierra Leone. This was a secret society involved in healing practices, and their medicine was kept in a house marked by painted spots on the outside walls. The figures were placed beside the medicine and consulted when necessary by the Yassi official.

Small packages and other things such as shells were added to scare away harmful spirits

AT AN OSHUN SHRINE
The Yoruba peoples of Nigeria worship many gods, one of which is the river god Oshun, the most important of the female gods. The myth of Oshun tells how the work of the male deities on Earth was unsuccessful until they included her in their ranks. Oshun is prayed to at her shrines (above) for female fertility and protection against disease.

THE PRESENCE OF ANCESTORS
Ancestor figures, such as those of the Yoruba, are regarded with great respect and are represented by both carvings (left) and masks, which are kept in houses and in shrines. Images of their followers (left) are part of everyday life, and their presence in homes illustrates the importance of life in the community. Such figures are carved by craftsmen according to established rules of design.

SANDE IN MASQUERADE
A Sande masquerader must conceal her identity, so she is completely covered by a wooden mask and long black raffia fringes (right). The characteristic black masks, although worn by the women, are always carved by men.

Typical elaborate hairstyle

Sande masquerade costume, Mende peoples, Sierra Leone

Folds of flesh around neck indicate wealth

Body is covered by raffia fringes

Traveler's charm, Zaire

SANDE WOMEN
The Sande society of the Mende of Sierra Leone is the only masking tradition performed by women in Africa. Each Sande society or lodge is controlled by senior officials led by a *sowei*, who is often the village midwife. Young girls are instructed in sexual, domestic, and craft skills in preparation for marriage and motherhood.

Medicine and healing

WHEN SEEKING A CURE for sickness, many Africans consult Western-style doctors and take advantage of modern technological treatments. However, the same people will also seek the advice of a traditional healer, a doctor of traditional medicine who is also a religious specialist. To identify the source of the illness, the healer often contacts good and evil spirits by going into a trance. Treatment may include an animal sacrifice, or, if another human being is considered responsible, the use of herbs or magical substances to combat the enemy spirit. The healer may also involve other people. Among the Ndembu of Zambia, friends of the patient are called together so that the healer can find out who among them is holding a grudge against the patient.

Birds symbolize the power of the elders

Wood splint to set fracture

Hook for extracting tonsils

Spatulas

Surgical knives

Nail heated to apply to wound

Bird-headed iron staffs, Yoruba, Nigeria

Counter-irritant

IRON STAFFS
In Yoruba society, medicine men belong to the cult of Osanyin, the god of herbal medicines. Osanyin's powers are secret, but are often represented by bird-headed staffs. The staffs are symbols of healing and herbalism. The central bird represents the power of the elders, who, after death, were believed to take the form of birds.

SURGICAL TOOLS FROM SOMALIA
These instruments reflect the curious mixture of outside influences (in this case, the Middle East) and traditional beliefs that occurs in African societies. As well as surgical tools to remove tonsils, spatulas, and a splint, there is also a counter-irritant that relies on the patient yelling when the heated nail is applied to the wound, letting the pain "escape by the mouth."

MAGICAL POWERS
This traditional healer in northern Cameroon is performing a healing ceremony. He involves the other villagers in making music by rhythmically passing a charm over the sick person. Healers often chant, sing, and dance in order to attract the goodwill of the spirits. They believe that this makes the medicines more effective, and encourages the patient to recover quickly.

Bag is made of woven raffia

Traditional healer's bag, Congo

Brass bell

TOOLS OF THE TRADE
As well as an ability to communicate with spirits, the healer has knowledge of local herbs and plants and the way they can be used in medicine. He also knows a great deal about his patients because he is a member of their community; as is the case with doctors all over the world, this often aids him in his work.

Bundle of shells and wood

Hippopotamus tooth

ESSENTIAL INGREDIENTS
The healer keeps his medicine bag with him at all times. Various items, such as wooden sticks and shells, are used in ceremonies that call upon the spirits in order to treat the patient. The medicine man understands the importance of a patient's mental or emotional condition, and how this may affect the ability to recover from an illness. The patient is therefore always treated in the community in which he or she lives, and is assured by the traditional healer of the community's concern and involvement, so that recovery can be encouraged.

Animal bone

Wooden sticks

Cowrie shell

Twisted pieces of tree root

Animal hooves

Bundle of sticks bound with string

Animal bone

A way of death

WHEN A PERSON DIES in Africa, the family sometimes performs a number of rituals to ensure that the spirit of the dead person moves easily into the world of his or her ancestors. Carvings of the ancestors, which are kept in shrines, help to retain the link between this world and the next, so the family does not lose contact. A period of mourning forges links between the living and the dead, and sometimes sets the family apart from the rest of society for a short time. In Madagascar, for example, women in mourning stop combing their hair and wear white.

Figure is made of wood covered in brass

FUNERARY FIGURES
Some funerary figures were carved to represent ancestors, whose remains were kept in containers in a special hut under the care of one of the male elders of the village. The carved figure was placed on top of the container. This Kota funerary figure from Gabon (above) would have been placed in a dark corner of the hut. The metal acts like a mirror and is believed to reflect back any evil that threatens.

ROYAL BURIAL
Kings and chiefs are considered sacred and have elaborate funerals. Traditionally, they are buried with their servants, who will help them in the afterlife. It was important that the kings were impressive in death, so they were often buried in full regalia. This man (left) was buried in a chamber in the ground, fully dressed and seated upright on a stool. He wore a copper crown and beaded armlets, and there were elephant tusks at his feet. His tomb was in the village of Igbo-Ukwu in Nigeria, and he was probably a ruler of the Ibo peoples.

VOICE DISGUISER
According to a legend, bones of one of the founding ancestors of the Tiv people of Nigeria were placed in a basket, and people were warned that if it was opened, crops would fail and the Tiv would perish. These ancestral bones have been replaced today by a priest using a voice disguiser as a warning to his people. Voice disguisers are used by many groups in Nigeria. They distort the priest's voice, making it boom.

Colored seeds decorate base

Abinsi voice disguiser, Nigeria

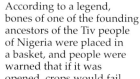

Graveposts are topped with carvings of animals, human figures, and nowadays even bicycles and airplanes

MEMORIALS IN MADAGASCAR
In Madagascar, dead people are placed in family tombs. Because many of the families are scattered, members often die far away from their family tombs. In such cases, the dead are temporarily buried somewhere else until there is enough money gathered for the ritual and all the relatives have been assembled. The body is then dug up, wrapped in a burial cloth, and reburied in the ancestral tomb. Tombs vary from region to region, and this circle of graveposts marks the tomb of someone of noble descent.

LUCKY FOR SOME
Some west African peoples regard the birth of twins as unfortunate, but the Yoruba of Nigeria welcome them and even consider them lucky after certain ritual duties have been completed. If one or both of the twins dies, a carving of them is made to ward off harmful spirits.

Funerary carvings of twins are called Ibeji

FINDING THE GUILTY CULPRIT
The Kuyu people of Gabon believe that the death of an individual is the result of an evil spell. The priest is called upon to detect the real cause of death by magical means. Wearing a long robe and a carved head (right), the priest dances among the male villagers. He stops dancing in front of the person believed responsible. That person simply accepts this and pays an appropriate fine.

This coffin was probably made for a fisherman

FANTASY COFFINS
Highly individual coffins are built on request in Ghana. A coffin with a large cocoa pod can be made for a cocoa farmer who wishes to take his wealth with him. The tradition began when a fisherman asked his nephew to make him a special coffin, as he hoped to go on fishing in the next world.

Ritual scars on cheeks

Sharpened teeth are typical of these carvings

Women and children are not allowed to see the head

Carved head, Kuyu people, Gabon

Nations at war

THERE WERE THREE DIFFERENT types of traditional warfare in Africa – state wars, raids by one group on another, and the jihads, or holy wars. The state wars were led by kings or emperors who were able to call their troops into battle on short notice. The king of Benin could raise 20,000 warriors in one day, and Ethiopian armies could number as many as 200,000. The raids were carried out by neighboring groups with different interests. The cattle-herding Maasai of Kenya, for example, were frequently at war with the farming Kikuyu in order to gain access to watering holes and land rights. Armies also went to war for religious purposes. The spread of Islam in the region south of the Sahara occurred partly because of trade but also as a result of the holy wars.

THE MAHDI
The Muslim leader Muhammed Ahmed was known as the Mahdi, or "the rightly guided one." He united many Sudanese peoples in a religious crusade in the second half of the 19th century.

Painted design and shape of shield tells us about the warrior

A victorious member of the ahosi *carries the head of an enemy*

WOMEN AT WAR
Although women sometimes accompanied their husbands to war, the king of Dahomey was exceptional in having an all-female guard. Called *ahosi*, they were greatly respected for their skill and bravery. They were not allowed to form any personal relationships, as they had to remain loyal to their king.

Maasai shield

MAASAI RAIDS
The Maasai of Kenya and their neighbors, the Kikuyu made frequent raids on each other. They planned their attacks carefully and used scouts to find out the whereabouts of cattle or other property belonging to the enemy. If two groups confronted one another, they often held a duel between their two best warriors before beginning the main combat.

FABRIC WAR TALES
Many stories of military campaigns were handed down through the generations. Dahomean chiefs or nobles would often commission clothmakers to make banners showing their successful battles.

Sudanese shield

PREPARING FOR WAR
Getting ready to go to war not only included planning strategies and tactics but also ritual preparations to strengthen the warrior and all his weapons. Many men, such as the Zulu soldiers, chewed magical substances and spat them in the direction of the enemy before attacking. Protective charms were also worn by either soldiers or their horses.

THE ZULUS AND CATTLE

The South African Zulu army was divided into regiments, each living in a self-sufficient village with its own herd of cattle. Each cow was chosen because its hide was the right regimental pattern and color. The hides were later made into shields. Zulu military strategy was even based on the shape of a cow. The young soldiers were the horns that encircled the enemy.

Supple pieces of hide are woven through slits to create pattern

Horse wearing cloth with Islamic text sewn on as protective charms

THE ASANTE

The kingdom of the Asante in Ghana rose to its height in the 18th century because of the power of its armies. These supported and protected its trade in gold and other products. The Asante's use of European firearms reduced their need for shields.

Zulu warriors wore elaborate headdresses of ostrich feathers

ZULU WARRIOR

Zulu regiments were distinguished by their elaborate headgear and shields. The more experienced soldiers had white shields with black markings; middle-rank soldiers held red shields; younger ones had black shields. The shields were made by specialists. King Shaka of the Zulus believed that, once dipped in water, the shields could protect his soldiers from heavy musket balls.

A detail from carved horn (right) showing British soldiers and Zulus

THE ZULU WARS

From the 17th century, Dutch farmers and their descendants, the Boers, had pushed gradually northward from the Cape of Good Hope in search of land and cattle. This led to battles with many groups that stood in their way. By the mid-1800s, they found themselves in conflict with the mighty army of the Zulu empire. It was not until the end of the century, when the British fought the Zulus with machine guns, that defeat signaled the end of an independent Zulu nation.

Hide was dried in the sun, buried under manure for two days, then pounded with stones

Zulu warshield

Carved buffalo horn showing scenes from the Zulu wars

Into battle

THE HORSEMEN of Sudanic Africa – the savanna region south of the Sahara Desert – played a vital role in the rise to power of many West African empires from the 9th century onwards. They controlled the trans-Saharan trade routes, and in this way acquired large North African horses to replace the smaller native breeds. The cavalry were divided into light and heavy squadrons. The light cavalry were usually mounted on small horses, armed with light javelins and one large spear, and rode bareback. In warfare, their speed and ability to maneuver meant that they could be used for surprise attacks on the enemy. A heavy cavalryman, whose uniform is shown on these pages, was usually mounted on a large horse, and armed with a sword, a heavy lance, a large shield, spears, and more protective armor. He formed part of the ruler's bodyguard.

Single-headed lance

THE QUILTED HORSEMAN
This is a lancer in the heavy cavalry of the Sultan of Bagirmi, drawn from life by an English major in the 1820s. Both rider and horse wore cloth as quilted armor to protect them from flying arrows. A double-headed lance was sometimes used in close combat with the enemy because it was capable of piercing metal armor.

Fulani body armour

Iron blade of battle ax forged

The ruler's bodyguards carried two spears

Ceremonial swords were worn across the body

Cuirass padded with leather for extra protection and comfort

Hand loop provides better grip

Heavy metal covering of body armor made of iron

HEAVY PROTECTION
A cuirass, or body armor, was worn by the Fulani heavy cavalryman as an alternative to chain mail. It was certainly better protection against arrows and spears than other methods of protection, such as the cloth that the Mossi cavalrymen of Burkina Faso wrapped around themselves. The Fulani horseman, weighted down by all this heavy armor, needed assistance to get onto his horse. If he fell off during a battle, he could not remount.

ARMED AND READY
The cavalryman carried several weapons into battle. The straight-bladed double-edged sword that he carried in its scabbard across his back was an essential weapon. However, his main weapons were his spears, because they were strong enough to pierce the chain mail of the enemy. Sometimes he carried an ax as well, which would have been hung from the saddle.

Birds' feathers were often used to decorate helmets

Today, metal parts are made from recycled containers when locally smelted iron is not available

Brightly colored cloaks were worn over the armor

DISTINCTIVE UNIFORM
Until the end of the 19th century, the Fulani heavy cavalryman wore metal body armour or chainmail under a quilted coat. After this, quilted coats, like the metal armor, were worn as part of the uniform only for ceremonies. The quilted armor consisted of separate pieces to cover different parts of the body. This particular horseman also wore a bright red cloak, its lining distinctively embroidered. The cloak was probably worn for warmth or in ceremonies, because in battle it would have been too cumbersome.

RECYCLED PROTECTION
As well as protecting the warrior in battle, this helmet was probably used for ceremonies, when the cavalryman appeared as part of his ruler's bodyguard. The helmet was padded with kapok (raw cotton) to protect the head from the metal headpiece.

Cloaks were sometimes embroidered or the lining was decorated to make them individual

Padded coat of raw cotton woven on a local loom

Cotton fringe hangs down back of neck

Heavy quilted coat was stuffed with kapok

Patchwork decoration was sometimes added on coat

Weapons and armor

OVER THOUSANDS OF YEARS, a huge variety of fighting implements has gradually evolved in Africa. Many of these weapons were used not only in battles and wars – different kinds of swords, spears, throwing knives, shields, and body armor were designed for display and ceremonial uses. For example, the *afena*, or state sword, is symbolic of the authority of the king of the Asante peoples of Ghana; the royal sword and lance are carried by the king of the Kuba people of Zaire on state occasions. Protection was provided not only by weapons and shields – Fulani and other Muslim warriors often wore sayings from the Koran, the holy book of Islam, for luck, encased in leather pouches hanging from the neck or sewn into clothes.

Battle-ax, Botswana

Iron knife, Mangbetu, Sudan

ALL SORTS OF SPEARS
Spears were frequently employed in both battle and hunting. The larger spear (left) was used by the Lango of Uganda, who frequently raided their neighbors to capture cattle. The smaller spear (far left) is a Zulu *iklwa* or thrusting spear, often used in close combat.

Hide is covered with velvet and silverwork

CLOSE COMBAT
Some of the deadliest and most effective weapons used during close combat were battle-axes. This ax from Botswana is decorated with incisions on the blade. Both the ax and the Sudanese knife were used as symbols of power.

Knobkerrie is also used as a swagger stick or snuff container

STATUS SYMBOL
An Ethiopian warrior had every reason to be proud of his shield, as it announced his status as well as his military skills. Wrapped in a red cotton cloth, the shield, along with the warrior's other arms, was carried on his mule. A servant boy stood behind his master during discussions and held the shield. Shields were often decorated with a lion's mane, tail, or paw, mounted in clasps of decorative silverwork.

ESSENTIAL ACCESSORY
The fighting stick was used by many peoples, including the Dinka of Sudan, as a throwing weapon, a fashionable accessory, a symbol of office, or simply as a tool for everyday tasks. Some sticks were spiked with metal studs and nails. Others had a socketed iron spike fixed to the end of the shaft. This spike was useful not only as an additional weapon in battle, but it could also be pushed into the ground to turn the stick into a stool.

DAGGERS AND KNIVES
African knives come in all shapes and sizes. This dagger from Nigeria was widely used by the armies south of the Sahara. It was attached to a soldier's arm by the leather strap. The copper knife, as with other copper weapons, was used mainly in ceremonial exchanges.

Dagger, Nigeria

Copper knife, Zaire

HUNGA-MUNGAS
Central African weapons are famous for their peculiar shapes, including this bird-headed throwing knife, called a hunga-munga until the 19th century. Both knives are shaped like bird's heads. The back of the "head" has a sharp spur, so that when the knife is thrown and fails to strike with the "beak," it impales with the edge of the spur instead. A soldier waited until he was close to the enemy, then took the knife from its sheath, throwing and spinning it like a boomerang.

Bird-headed throwing knife, Gabon

Throwing knife, Congo

Copper bells on neck charm to keep horse and rider safe in battle

Tassels on headpiece protect horse's face from flies

QUILTED COAT
Traditionally worn by the horsemen of Sudanic Africa, the savanna region south of the Sahara, fabulous horse costumes are still used in ceremonial displays today. This Fulani horse armor is made from quilted cotton cloth stuffed with kapok – the silky hairs that surround the seeds of the silk cotton tree. In full battle armor, the horse would also have been protected from a rain of arrows or spears by chain mail or leather pieces across the flanks. A helmet, made of bound rags and often covered in chain mail, completed the outfit.

Cotton fabric is quilted with strong cotton thread

Girth strap ties around horse's stomach

Metal stirrup attaches to saddle with leather strap

Barter and exchange

Arab traders could cross 200 miles (320 km) of desert in a week

TRADE ROUTES ACROSS THE SAHARA
Caravan routes used by Muslim merchants linked the towns at the southern edge of the Sahara desert with parts of North Africa by way of oasis towns such as Walata, the market town on the northern border of the Mali empire. Timbuktu became a prosperous trading city and a center of learning.

FOR CENTURIES, AFRICANS have traded in the rich resources of their continent. The trading routes that developed across the Sahara Desert during the first millenium A.D. helped to establish the great empires of the Songhay, Mali, and ancient Ghana. In the 15th and 16th centuries, Portuguese sailors opened up the sea routes to eastern Africa, and Muslim merchants began to carry goods by camel to and from West Africa across the Sahara. Gold and copper, mined in southern and western Africa, were transported to the East African coast, the Middle East, and Asia. Salt, ivory, ebony, kola nuts, and later slaves, were exchanged for ceramics, beads, silk, and cowrie shells from Europe and eastern Asia.

Trading ship, called a dhow, used by Muslim traders in the Persian Gulf

Triangular lateen sails would be unfurled to catch monsoon winds

Zebra illustrated in watercolor and gold on paper by the Indian artist Mansur

TRADING EAST
Gifts such as this zebra were brought to the court of the Indian Moghul emperor Jehangir in the 17th century. Traders from the East African coast crossed the Indian Ocean, linking the markets of East Africa with the Red Sea, the Persian Gulf, India, and the Far East.

TRADING SHIPS
The Indian Ocean was fairly easy to navigate because of the monsoon winds that blow steadily toward the African coast during the winter months, and away from it, toward India, during the summer. This allowed regular trading of goods by sailing ships to and from East Africa. All along the East African coast, towns such as Zanzibar, Kilwa, and Mombasa grew and developed as they became major trading centers.

TRAVELING IN A CARAVAN
Traders were only able to travel such distances across the Sahara because of the remarkable staying power of the camel. This extraordinary animal can travel for days without food or water because of its body's ability to conserve water and store fat. Caravans with as many as 12,000 camels would journey for up to three months across the desert.

Brass manillas were melted and used to make Benin bronzes

Currency

Before the introduction of western coinage, many other means of payment were used – animals, textiles, beads, as well as other objects considered precious. In traditional Africa, currencies varied widely from region to region. Among the cattle-herding communities, the number of cattle owned by a person indicated his wealth, and the cattle were used for trading. In other areas, locally woven cloths were used, as well as spears, beads, bars of salt, cowrie shells, and metal bars known as manillas.

Manillas, the most valuable money unit in ancient Benin

CURRENCY AND EXCHANGE RATES
Before the introduction of scrap metal and western coinage, locally produced metal was an extremely important item of exchange in Africa. Iron money took the form of objects such as arrowheads, hoes, or spears, and in north Zaire and some parts of Sudan, throwing knives (pp. 46–47). Among the Nkutshu of Zaire two currency blades could usually buy a bride. Each was worth 1,250 of the smaller hoe heads.

Widely used in north Africa

African elephant on base of coin

Used as gold standard for trading

Hoe head currency, central Africa

Austrian Maria Theresa dollar, late 1700s

English gold guinea, 1660s

Almoravid gold dinar, 1100s

Salt bars were exported to Arabia and the Far East

DINKA WEDDING NEGOTIATIONS, SUDAN
In the cattle-herding areas of Africa, the family of the prospective husband are expected to make a payment to the family of the future bride. This bride price is traditionally in the form of cattle. Here, the families are negotiating the bride price. The sticks on the ground represent the number of cattle.

Metal spear paid as bride price, Azande, Sudan

Copper ring weighing nearly 6.5 lbs (3 kg) "bought" one wife, central Africa

49

A slave's journey

As THE TOBACCO, SUGAR, and cotton plantations became established in the Caribbean and the Americas, the plantation owners needed more workers. European traders were interested in capturing or buying slaves from Africa, and African rulers were willing to sell the slaves they had captured in wars. Men, women, and children were forcibly taken, tied, or shackled together, and marched to the coast to await a ship. Those who survived the long journey were sold to plantation owners.

DETERRENTS TO SLAVERY
These lip disks (for both top and bottom lips) were worn by the Sara women of central Africa. Although considered attractive by the Sara peoples, the lip disks were not considered an asset by the Europeans. This made it less likely that the women would be captured and marched across Africa to be transported and sold.

Lack of space meant that slaves could not lie down

ECONOMIC DISASTER
From 1500 to 1850, about 25 million people either died during wars fought between African rulers or were captured and sold into slavery, like this netted man awaiting transport. This had a disastrous effect on traditional ways of life, and deprived the continent of a vital part of the population.

TRAVELING ON A SLAVESHIP
Slaveships were usually overloaded, with as many as 600 slaves crammed into a space built for 400. Many slaves died on the way, and some committed suicide by refusing food or throwing themselves overboard to drown.

The boys' room – men and boys were kept at the front of the boat

SHACKLED
Gangs of armed raiders traveled into the forests of western Africa to capture as many men, women, and children as possible. The villagers were shackled together and marched to the coast. During the journey they were treated with great brutality, and at the coast the hardship continued. Although children were often captured with their parents, the traders were not concerned if families or villagers were kept together. They separated the slaves according to age, size, sex, and physical fitness.

NO WAY OUT
On a slaveship, limited space and the poor ventilation and sanitation led to many deaths, both from sickness and suicide. Sometimes the slaves mutinied, but this usually led to the ringleaders being killed, or the slaves wandering the ocean, unable to steer the captured ship.

BRANDS AND BRANDING
The slave traders cared little for their slaves, merely wanting them to survive to be sold in reasonable condition. They branded the slaves as if they were cattle before they were put on board. After auction, the slaves were branded again by the plantation owner to show that they were his property.

SLAVE AUCTIONS
When the slaves had been safely landed on the shores of Virginia in the United States, or in the Caribbean, they were sold at auction. Plantation owners and managers inspected every individual to see if he or she was healthy before they would bid – they examined the teeth in particular as a guide to age. Slaves were not regarded as people but as something to be replaced if they got old or ill, or showed signs of rebellion.

The auctioneer sells a family into slavery

Symbol for a slave

HUMAN CARGO
Slaves were regarded as cargo along with other products, and were identified on the ship's list by a special symbol (left).

THE RISE AND FALL OF SLAVERY
Arabic traders began the widespread selling of Africans as slaves over 1,000 years ago, contact with Europeans increased the trade, and it was at its height by 1800. The slaves' endurance of frequent whippings and beatings prompted anti-slavery movements in the U.S. and England as early as 1690. In England the anti-slavery movement gained influence and momentum throughout the 18th century. In 1833, British Parliament passed a law that freed all slaves the following year. In the United States, slavery was abolished in the North by the 13th Amendment after the Civil War.

Slave-driver's whip, west coast, Africa

Whips were usually made of hemp

Most slaves were aged between 16 and 45

Model of the slave ship *Brookes* used by William Wilberforce to campaign against slavery in the British Houses of Parliament

In the men's room, the strongest men were permanently chained in twos

Women's room – women were set free to exercise and eat, but manacled otherwise

The slaves were fed rice, corn, yams, cassava, and beans

The officers' cabin was over the women's quarters

The girls, branded like the rest, were kept at the back of the boat

Crafts and skills

IN MANY AFRICAN SOCIETIES, some activities are carried out solely by women, and others are performed only by men. This is particularly the case with two highly skilled occupations – pottery and metalworking. Pottery is made by women for everyday use, but it is also used in many initiation ceremonies for young girls. The Yoruba of Nigeria and the Shona of Zimbabwe use pottery items as part of a new bride's belongings. Metalworking is an exclusively male activity. Because of his technical skill, handed down from family to family, the blacksmith is respected, feared, or even despised by other villagers.

Human-headed pot, Azande, Sudan

Wooden mallet to pound clay

Bark of allogia tree, when soaked, produces red dye to color finished pot

Stone to polish molded pot after it has dried in the sun

New pot is begun on flat piece of old pot

Shell for smoothing and removing surplus clay before drying

IN HUMAN FORM
In the early 20th century, potters of the Mangbetu people of northeastern Zaire and the Azande people of Sudan began to produce pots in the form of human heads, and sometimes the entire body. This form was probably made largely for sale to Europeans.

POTTERY TOOLS
Clay is a very versatile material. It is easy to manipulate and can be used to make a wide variety of shapes. Only simple tools are needed, like these, which belonged to a potter in Sudan. They are used to make coil pots from rolls of clay placed on top of each other and then smoothed.

Earthenware nozzle to direct air onto fire

Fibrous root to apply dye while pot is still hot

MAKING A POT
In most African societies, it is the women who produce pottery, and they make it by hand. In North Africa, however, male potters use a potter's wheel. A kiln for firing is also used only in North Africa. Elsewhere, the pottery may be fired by covering with brushwood or grass and setting it alight. A wide variety of items are produced, such as pipes, toys, furniture, and jewelry, as well as containers. For the most part, the women make everyday items for use or sale. However, there are some established artisans, such as the potters of Bida in Nigeria.

Ironworking

Iron was produced at a number of sites south of the Sahara Desert from as early as 300 B.C. The iron ore was heated to a high temperature in an earthenware furnace. The smelting produced a "bloom," a lump of raw iron that was fashioned into ingots, or bars. This was then forged by local smiths, or traded to other smiths in distant communities. Smelting iron was a difficult process. Often before it began, there was a ritual ceremony followed by music and dancing to ensure its success.

Finished hoe blade

Iron hoe blade emerging

Blade is fastened to long pole for use in the fields

FORGING IRON
Smiths are considered mysterious and powerful figures, set apart from the rest of the community. To maintain secrecy, Tuareg smiths even speak a different language, Tenet, to fellow smiths.

Bloom, or raw iron

Bloom beaten flat

SHAPING A HOE BLADE
Some smiths specialize in making one type of metal object – for example, knives, swords, spears, or hoes. Raw iron or imported scrap metal is heated until it can be pounded into the rough shape of the object – in this case, a hoe blade. Until the 19th century, hoe blades were a form of currency as well as an agricultural tool.

Wooden stick worked by apprentice's right hand to pump air into hide pouches

Wooden stick worked by apprentice's left hand

TOOLS OF THE TRADE
The smith's equipment consists of hammers, chisels, an anvil, and bellows. Air is pumped through the bellows by the smith's apprentice or a young male member of the family. This air controls the fire, and therefore the temperature at which the metal is heated. The hot metal is beaten into shape on the anvil with a hammer. The smith frequently returns the metal to the fire until the task is completed. Although the tools used are simple, some metal objects produced are very sophisticated, particularly weaponry such as the extraordinary bird-headed throwing knives of Gabon (pp. 46-47).

Hide pouch that fills with air

The lost-wax process

IN THE 1660S, THE FIRST Dutch explorers of the west coast of Africa described the extraordinary kingdom of Benin. They were particularly impressed by the plaques and bronze works created by Benin craftsmen to decorate the Oba's palace. The Benin portraits, usually of royal figures, were cast by the lost-wax process, which is described here. The head of the Queen Mother of Benin is re-created by the traditional method. This technique is also found along the coast in Ghana, where the Asante used it to make gold weights (pp. 56–57).

1 MAKING THE CORE
The core, a mixture of loamy soil (clay, silt, and sand) and water, is built up from the base gradually. Each stage is allowed to dry so it will be strong enough to support the weight above. The core is then covered with a 0.1 in layer of beeswax, which is the eventual width of the bronze.

Detail put on with molding bone

2 MOLDING THE WAX
Having completely covered the core with a smooth layer of beeswax, the craftsman begins to etch the pattern and decoration with a molding bone. The color of the wax varies according to the diet of the bees that produce it.

3 SEALING THE CORE
The head is now covered in the same loamy mixture that formed the core. This is done in three layers. The first, the layer nearest the head, has to be very well worked and smooth, and is left to dry thoroughly. The other two layers are put on to give support and strength to the mold. String is put between the last two layers to hold the mold in position in case it breaks while being fired.

Etched wax

Very smooth, loamy first layer

4 READY TO FIRE
When the head has been completely sealed with the three layers of loamy soil, it is ready to fire. Sticks are put in all over the head to hold the mold in position once the wax has melted. The mold is either surrounded by wood and fired above ground, or put in a pit and wood arranged around the head is set on fire.

The layers follow the shape of the mold

Completed first layer of loamy soil

Sharp knife to trim

Bone modeling tool

Metal modeling tool

Wax is built up inside the base to form a channel, so that when the wax melts, it can flow out

Crucible containing molten bronze

Wood held in place by wire, which is gradually tightened to keep wood hot

Shield to protect from heat

The bronze has to be heated until it is orange-hot, which is hotter than red-hot

6 POURING THE BRONZE

The bronze is now heated until it runs freely. The next stage is a crucial – and dangerous – part of the process. The orange-hot bronze is carefully poured into the upside-down mold, where it fills the gap left by the wax. The mold is left in the sand to cool until it can be handled. It is then dug out and the outer layers broken off with a hammer to reveal the newly cast bronze head beneath.

The finished replica head of the Queen Mother of Benin

This stage is not complete until all the wax has flowed out

5 FIRING THE MOLD

The wood burning around the mold causes the wax to melt, and it runs out through a channel in the bottom of the mold. This creates a vacuum where the wax has been. When all the wax has run out, the hot mold is buried upside-down in sand.

BENIN "BRONZES"

Strictly speaking, the mixture of copper, zinc, lead, and tin used to make Benin "bronzes," like this 17th-century staff mount, resulted in not bronze but brass. However, they are usually referred to as Benin bronzes. Because the metals were rare, some early bronzes are only 0.03 in thick. Later on, the people of Benin traded with the Europeans to obtain brass manillas (pp. 48-49), which they melted down.

7 FINAL TOUCHES

The head is now left to cool. Then the base is cut off with a sharp blade. Next the artist digs out the core, using a hammer and chisel. The loamy soil will come out easily from the now-blackened core. This difficult method of casting made possible the creation of very delicate bronze works of art.

Gold of the Asante

Asante gold weight

ALTHOUGH THE ORIGINS of gold-working in Africa are uncertain, western Africa supplied Europe with large quantities of gold before the discovery of the Americas. European nations gained so much wealth from trade with that region, then called Guinea, that the gold coins the British minted were named guineas. Gold was obtained by washing soil on riverbeds and banks, or by digging it from pits. The gold ranged in size from fine, granular gold dust to sizeable pieces, or nuggets. In Asante, Ghana, larger gold nuggets were given to the king, the Asantehene. The goldsmiths were a privileged class in Asante society, and used the lost-wax process (pp. 54–55) to produce delicately designed gold and brass pieces.

The scales were handheld

GOLD DUST
Gold dust was, until the 20th century, the main form of currency among the Asante. Weights made of brass, but often called gold weights and cast in many different shapes, were made to measure out units of gold dust. The dust was weighed in a set of scales, using a spoon. Weights were also used as jewelry and as charms by storytellers.

Gold weights

Set of scales

CEREMONIAL GOLD
The ceremonial daggers, trophy head, finger rings, and bird ornament (right) are part of the treasure of King Kofi-Karikari, who was Asantehene from 1867 to 1875. They are decorated with, or cast in, virgin gold – gold in its natural state. They were never intended for use in war, but would have been carried when the king appeared in public on ceremonial occasions.

Spoon to measure gold dust

Gold dust box

WEIGHING OUT THE GOLD
To carry out a transaction, the gold weight of a buyer had to be weighed against that of a seller. If both weights were equal, the buyer measured out the agreed amount of gold dust onto his scales, and this was then transferred to the seller's scales for confirmation. If both agreed on the weighing, the seller took the gold dust and the buyer the goods.

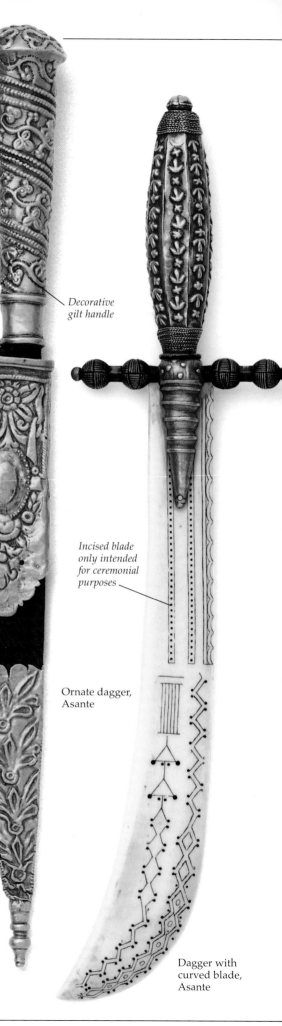

Decorative gilt handle

Incised blade only intended for ceremonial purposes

Ornate dagger, Asante

Dagger with curved blade, Asante

THE NATURAL WORLD TAKING SHAPE

Asante gold ornaments are often shaped like animals, birds, fish, insects, and fruit. The goldsmiths used the lost-wax process because it enabled them to achieve complicated shapes. When the mold had been cracked open, they scrubbed the ornament in water mixed with lime juice to clean it and make the gold shine.

Bird ornament from stool of state, Asante

Wood carving covered with gold leaf

ON PARADE
Asante ceremonies have changed very little for hundreds of years. They are very colorful. The chiefs dress in their finest clothes, wear gold crowns and jewelry, and carry ceremonial staffs. The Asantehene is carried on a stool of state, and protected, like the chiefs, by a sunshade.

Head weighs over 3 lbs (1.5 kg)

Ornament is one of a pair that would have been attached to the arms of the stool of state

HEADS OF GOLD

Sometimes the goldsmiths would cast a head in gold. This delicately cast head, together with the other gold objects on these pages, was part of the Asante treasure taken as booty by the British from Kumasi in 1874, after they had defeated the Asante. The head represents a chief killed in battle, and may be either King Worosa of Banda or King Adinkra of Gyaman. Gold heads often appeared on the royal throne, or were attached to the ceremonial swords that often played an important part in rituals.

Delicate decorative gold work

Rings were often decorated with flowers

ASANTE FINGER RINGS
The Asante impressed the first European visitors to their country by the colorful nature of their ceremonies and the large number of gold ornaments that they wore. The chiefs wore many gold crowns, bracelets, and pendants. The hands of the Asantehene were always adorned with large rings when he appeared at official festivals.

Trophy head, Asante

Masks and masquerade

IN SUB-SAHARAN AFRICA, masks are used for many different social events and rituals. They are worn with a costume that often hides the real identity of the wearer. The role of most masks is to discipline, or educate, or inform, or lend authority. The role is communicated through movement and dance. One mask may perform several functions at the same time, or several masks may play the same role in a ceremony. Sometimes, masks can be worn purely to entertain.

Colors are made from vegetable dyes

Band to hold mask on head made from woven raffia

Fringe made from raffia

The mask is made from branches and beaten bark

OGONI MASK, NIGERIA
Once a masquerader puts on a mask, he or she is transformed, or assumes the spirit of the character of the mask. The masker then becomes a communication link between the real and the supernatural world. Many masks are designed to look like animals. This Ogoni mask is one of those worn by young men, who perform athletic displays in imitation of the animals they represent.

CHOKWE MASK, ANGOLA
The Chokwe people have a rich masking tradition. Their masks are divided into three groups called Mukishi, based on the spirits that they represent. This mask is worn by the man directing the male initiation ceremonies, when boy children pass from childhood into adulthood. Boys spend several months at a school in the bush, learning to be adults and undergoing tests of endurance. Sometimes, the masks are burned at the end of the ritual.

Cowrie shells sewn onto textile made of vegetable fibers

KUBA MASK, ZAIRE
The Mashamboy masks of the Kuba peoples of Zaire were ordered to be made by the king because a spirit called the Mwaash a Mbooy was terrorizing his people. The mask was meant to look like the spirit and was worn only by the chiefs to enforce discipline.

Dyed raffia fringe covered the shoulders of the Kuba masquerader

BAMILEKE MASK, CAMEROON

The Bamileke are a large group of farming people who live on volcanic plateaus in the southern Cameroon grasslands of West Africa. This group is divided into secret societies or brotherhoods, each of which has its own masks and musical instruments. Although the mask is based on the human face and head, it has exaggerated features. The elongated shape, the full cheeks, and the distorted mouth emphasize the large size of the face; they represent the supernatural and set the mask, and its wearer, apart from the human world.

Even the ears of this Bamileke mask are exaggerated in size

Parallel lines represent the weave of the cloth of a cap or hat

Wooden mask is first covered with red ocher, then the stripes made with chalk and soot

The masks were worn on the top of the head

Birds' feathers are often used to make masks more elaborate

GELEDE MASKS, NIGERIA

In traditional Yoruba society, women are considered to have two distinct sides to their natures – they have the ability to create new life, and they have the potential for great destruction. The Gelede masquerade, danced in male pairs or female pairs, is supposed to ensure that women's power is channeled for the benefit of the community. There are many different designs of Gelede mask.

WEARING A MASK

Many masks are worn over the face. A large number, however, such as the Gelede masks above, are designed to be worn on top of the head. The bird-headed mask that completes this masquerade costume from Cameroon is worn like this. It adds greatly to the height and deliberately imposing presence of the masquerader.

At an annual festival, mask is worn with cloth to cover body and ankle rattles

Musical instruments

EARLY AMPLIFIERS
Hanging under the keys of this xylophone are gourds – the dried, hollow shells of fruit from the gourd or squash plant. These amplify the sound of the player hitting the keys, producing a rich, resonant tone. Xylophones are played with other instruments on their own – and in northwest Ghana, for example, for making special announcements to the village.

MUSIC IS EVERYWHERE in Africa. Musical instruments and song are a basic part of the African way of life, from a mother singing a lullaby to her newborn baby to elaborate village festivals full of color and costumes. People may use music to break up the monotony of the working day. A farmer, for example, might sing a song to encourage his crops during hoeing and sowing. In rural areas, herders and hunters scattered over vast distances signal each other by blowing coded musical messages into a flute. Some music, such as that of warrior groups, or beer-drinking and hunting songs, can be performed only by men. Other music is sacred to women only, and might be played during rites of passage into adulthood, or during childbirth. The enormous variety of musical instruments across Africa ranges from elaborately carved ceremonial drums to the most basic of rattles, made only from pieces of scrap metal or bits of bark.

Bells held in the air by handle

DOUBLE BELLS
Musicians play these double bells by holding them up and striking the two metal cones with sticks, rods, or horns. Bells such as these are used mainly as percussion instruments at festivals and masquerades. This bell set comes from Cameroon in West Africa.

HAND-HELD PIANO
A sansa is an instrument that works like a tiny hand-held piano. Narrow metal or wooden strips are arranged over a sounding board and attached to a resonator gourd. The musician plucks the metal strips, each of which corresponds to a note, with his thumbs. These thumb-pianos are often called the "traveler's friend," because people can play them while wandering from place to place. This one is used by the Umbundu peoples of Angola.

Dried, hollowed-out gourds act as resonators

STRING ALONG
This musical bow from Cameroon is simply a wooden stick across which strings have been tightly stretched. The strings are bowed, plucked, struck, or hit with a bow, which is usually a flexible piece of wood with a string attached at both ends. Gourds, made from hollowed-out, dried squashes amplify the very soft sounds made by the strings. A musician can coax a whole range of sounds from the bow by holding it at different angles to his body – for example, against his chest.

Decorative cowrie shells around mouthpiece

Strips of hide are wrapped around carved wood

Single-membrane drum, Congo

Membrane is stretched across top of drum and secured with wooden pegs

HIGH LIFE MUSIC
High life is popular all over Africa, as well as in Europe. It is based on the traditional music of Ghana and Sierra Leone, but has been influenced by regimental band music, sea shanties, church hymns, Latin American music, and calypso. Today, the main instruments used are acoustic guitar and vocals.

"Hourglass" drum is shaped so it can be tucked under player's arm

LUTE
The harp lute, or kora, is one of the most beautiful of all African instruments, and is typical of the Mali region. A gourd, cut in half and covered with cow skin, is used as a resonator. The musician rests the gourd against his body and plucks the strings with his thumbs and forefingers.

Leather thongs secure strings to wooden neck

Long neck is pointed away from body during play

Pressure drum and beater, Cameroon

ALL SORTS OF DRUMS
African drums range from the simplest skin aprons stretched over cooking pots to elaborate instruments used for masquerades. Some drums are small enough to be tucked under one arm (above); others (right) are almost as tall as the drummer. The drum is usually carved out of a solid piece of wood, or strips of wood bound together by iron hoops. Children often make toy drums from old cans and oil drums, or from the hard shells of fruit.

Strings are often made of horse hair

Mouthpiece is made out of a piece of gourd

Animal hide is often used to decorate

BLOWN FROM THE SIDE
This extraordinary side-blown trumpet is played by the Madi people of Uganda. Usually made from wood or animal horn, trumpets such as these have many uses. As well as being played simply for the fun of listening to music, they are used to convey messages and signals from village to village.

Although very long, wooden trumpet is not heavy

Masquerade performed

MASKED DANCE, or masquerade, is performed in many communities in western and central Africa, and plays an important part in rituals and social events. Once inside the costume, the identity of the masquerader is hidden from other people, and he or she takes on the character represented by the mask. Often parts of the body are exaggerated with padding or pieces of wood. Combined with dance steps, gestures, songs, and sounds, the complete costume becomes a powerful and energetic force that represents the spirit world as well as the world of humans. Masquerade is mainly performed by men who are members of secret societies.

Ibo masquerade costume, Nigeria

Headdress of carved and painted wood

Colorful, hand-embroidered cloth is a feature of this costume

DANCE STAFF, NIGERIA
This iron staff (left) is used by the Yoruba people in a masquerade to celebrate Ogun, god of iron and blacksmiths, carvers, and all those who use metal instruments.

AN ANNUAL EVENT
The masquerade happens at specific times and to celebrate certain events, such as harvest, or the initiation of children to adulthood. The costume may only be used for a short time – maybe only a week or a month. Afterward it is stored away until it is needed the following year. This masquerade costume is worn by Ibo men, who imitate young girls as part of the annual harvest celebration.

BODY DECORATION
Young girls of the Mbuti people of Zaire are painted with white as part of a ceremony to announce their status as young women. Colored paints are often put on the body, usually of a young person, in many different ceremonies. Paints, like the costumes, disguise the wearer and add to the power and mystery of the ceremony.

Serrated design

DANCE SHIELD, KENYA
In the ceremonial performances of the Kikuyu people, dance shields, called *ndome*, are worn on the upper left arm by young men. The serrated design on the inside of the shield is always the same. The outer design varies according to the age of the men and the region in which they live.

MASKED DANCERS, MALI
Among the Dogon of Mali, the men's secret society, Awa, controls and organizes all funeral events. The masks (left) are worn at rituals in which the prestige of a deceased person and his descendants is enhanced by masked performance and generous hospitality.

Dancers appear in procession at funerals

Carved wooden headdress covered with fiber

INITIATION CEREMONY, ANGOLA
A boy of the Chokwe peoples goes through a set process to mark his transition to manhood. This involves living with other initiates in a secluded camp some way from the village, for a month, being circumcized, and being educated in the social and moral values of the community. This feared costume (right) represents the spirit of deceased chiefs and heroes, and is worn by the supervisor. Afterward the boy returns to the village as a "new man."

Face and identity of wearer completely hidden by mask

Metal-tipped spear

Leg rattles, Cameroon

Metal rattles attached to tie made from grass fibers

MUSIC AND SOUND
Masquerades are exciting and noisy occasions accompanied by constant drumming. Flywhisks, amulets, and sometimes weapons are brandished by the dancing masquerader. Leg rattles tied around his ankles shake furiously as the masquerader moves energetically. Drums, rattles, and the sounds made by the masquerader help to create atmosphere and drama.

Ceremonial ax of wood and metal

Drum is carved from a whole log

Slit drum and beaters, Sudan

Skirt made from grass fibers

Index

Acknowledgments

Dorling Kindersley would like to thank:
Gavin Durrant; Jason Slater for photographic assistance; Exeter City Museums and Art Gallery, Royal Albert Memorial Museum, Exeter, Devon (Jane Burkinshaw, Graham Searle, John Allen); the Powell-Cotton Museum, Birchington, Kent (Derek and Sonia Howlett, Malcolm Harman); the Royal Pavilion, Art Gallery and Museum, Brighton, Sussex (Anthony Shelton); Robert Mucci 27tr; Central St Martins College of Art and Design (David Reed, Aron Macartney); the Commonwealth Institute (Yvette Fields), the Trustees of the Wallace Collection, London (David Edge), C. J. Spring; Ubersee-Museum Bremen, Germany 34br.

Design and editorial assistance Mark Haygarth, Joseph Hoyle, Ivan Finnegan, Susan St. Louis, Helena Spiteri and Gin von Noorden.
Models: Wisdom Omoda Omodamwe – Lost wax process pp.54-55; Len Snell (Thorp Modelmakers, London) – Botswana house pp.12-13.
Additional special photography: Andy Crawford (pp.12-13).
Artwork: Jason Lewis, John Woodcock, Luigi Gallante.

Picture credits
(t=top b=bottom c=centre l=left r=right a=above)
Musée Nationale des Arts Africains / Réunion des Musées Nationaux 42br; British Library 31tr;

Trustees of the British Museum 12bl; Jean-Loup Charmet 31tr, 32tl, 50c, 50bl; James Davis Travel Photography 22tr, 28c, 29cl, 29br; Robert Estall / Carol Beckwith and Angela Fisher 41bl; Mary Evans Picture Library 25tl, 43tc, 43tr, 44tl, 51cl; Werner Foreman Archive 11br, 12br, 53tr; Robert Harding Picture Library 6bl, 6tr, 7bl, 8bl, 9tr, 9b, 16bc, 17bc, 18tl, 26cr, 27br, 32c, 59br, 60tl; Michael Holford 6cl, 40tr; Collection Photothèque du Musée de L'Homme 50tr; Hutchinson Library 7tl, 8c, 9tl, 10tr, 11tl, 13tr, 14tr, 16tr, 17tr, 18cl, 21tl, 21tc, 22cl, 23tl, 23br, 26cl, 28cr, 33br, 37tc, 37c, 40br, 46bc, 49cl, 49bl, 52bc, 57tl, 63tl; Jak Kilby 61tl; Magnum Photos / S. Perkins 7c, / Abbas 15br, Thomas Hoepker 25br, / Abbas 26tl, / Ian Berry 26bl, / Fred

Mayer 30br, / C. Steele Perkins 31c; Mansell Collection 42tr; National Maritime Museum 48br; Panos Pictures 8tr, 33bl; Pitt Rivers Museum 40l; the Trustees of the Powell-Cotton Museum Trust 24tr; Rex Features 7cr; Telegraph Colour Library / Colorific / Jim Pickerill 10c, / Mirella Riccardi 19cl, / Cosmos 19tr, / Richard Wilkie 20bl, / Lawrence Manning 20c, / Terry Fincher 24cr, 34c, 41tl, / Contact Press 62cl; Victoria and Albert Museum 48cl; Wilberforce House, Hull City Museums and Art Galleries 50-51, 51tl, 51tr; Zefa Pictures 15tl, 23cr, 38br, 39tr.
Every effort has been made to trace the copyright holders of photographs. The publishers apologize for any unavoidable omissions.